INTRODUCTION

Hello to you all.

You may have read some of my other revision guides - GCSE English Language, and An Inspector Calls.

If so, that's great! I hope they were helpful.

If not, do check them out, as I think they might be useful to you (unless you aren't studying An Inspector Calls, in which case, you're welcome to buy it but it will be pretty useless to you).

This guide to Macbeth will I hope give you a fresh perspective on what is one of the most extraordinary pieces of literature in the history of, well, literature.

I'll dig a little into Shakespeare's background (just enough to enable you to understand the background to the man and why he wrote the play). I'll talk about the historical context at the time the play was written and when it was set. And at the end I'll give you some ideas as to how you might go about approaching the exam questions.

And that's it! All pretty simple. It may seem rather a daunting play, but actually it isn't. Yes, Shakespeare's language can be offputting at first, but once you get into it I hope you'll see how beautiful it is.

It's actually the reason I became a teacher! When I studied it aged 15 I was blown away by how powerful it was. And it's always been my favourite play to teach.

Let's get started!

WHY LEARNING ENGINEERS?

Bit of a strange name, isn't it? What has engineering got to do with learning English? Look at it this way: every text you study, whether it's a novel, play, poem or piece of non fiction, has its own set of moving parts. This might be how language is used, the way in which the words are structured, or perhaps punctuation.

A writer's job is a little like an engineer's in that they have to take these parts and mesh them together so they work really well. Cogs and levers on their own are useless, in the same way that all the words in a dictionary don't make a work of genius.

The texts you study have been crafted by those who have really mastered these arts. And it's your job to take these literary 'engines' apart and explain how they work.

So when we talk about engineering we don't mean oil and cogs, or wires and circuitboards. We mean words, sentences, punctuation, and so on.

You'll notice that the approach I take when structuring these guides is to follow the process and learner engineer would take when mastering their craft.

We first of all look at the story, play or poem engine, listen to it, try to get a sense of how and why it works.

We will then take it apart, piece by piece, and examine each of these parts to understand how it fits into the broader whole. How character fits into setting, or how certain characters might use certain language or be described in a certain way.

Just make sure you have an oily rag handy to wipe your hands down afterwards!

MACBETH: GCSE STUDY GUIDE

DETAILED, ADVANCED AND IN-DEPTH: FOR ANYONE WHO WANTS TO TARGET THE TOP GRADES!

DARREN COXON

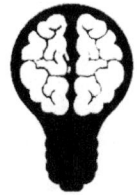

A NOTE BEFORE WE START

Before we get cracking, let me give you some advice (I am a teacher so I am allowed).

When you read through this guide, have a paper copy of the play open in front of you and a pencil. Not a pen. A pencil. As you read, underline things and make notes in the margin of the play.

I like to think of my guides as me beside you when you read, pointing out interesting or useful things and gently suggesting you make a note of them. This is what I do in the classroom so I see no reason to change things as it's quite effective and I've got very good results over the years.

You may go to one of those schools that has issued all their students iPads. And this is fine: my school was actually the first in the country whose 6th form was issued with them (that was a long time ago). And so you may have the play on the iPad.

But when you read the book I would recommend grabbing a paper copy and a pencil. This isn't just because I am old-fashioned (remember, I've been using iPads since before you moved up to senior school).

It's because it's simply a better way to revise - pencil notes in the play are a really good way to record your initial thoughts. You can then transfer them to flash cards or whatever revision technique you find most useful.

However, if all you have is an e-copy it's also ok: if you're able to highlight and annotate on the screen all the better. I do think it's important to find some way of recording the things you learn in this guide. As there is quite a lot to take in!

HOW THIS GUIDE IS SET OUT

The **first section** will take you act by act through the play. This should give you a detailed overview of the plot, and will touch on character and theme.

The **second section** will dive into characters, going much deeper into their function in the play. It is worth saying from the start that characters are nothing more than one of the ingredients of a story. They serve a function, a purpose. They are not real people (even if they might be based on historical figures). More on that later.

The **third section** will go into themes in a bit more detail. This is probably the most complex section in the book, but do give it a go even if you're only aiming for a Grade 4 or 5 in your exam.

The **fourth section** will say a little about form and structure, as it's important that you write about the play *as a play*.

The **final section** will take a few different types of exam question and give you some ideas as to how to answer them. It will also give you some exemplar answers and will suggest how you can take your notes and turn them into useful revision materials.

No time to lose: let's dive in.

BACKGROUND TO THE PLAY

HISTORICAL CONTEXT

The play *Macbeth* was written at the start of the 1600s, which was an interesting time in British history. Most of Shakespeare's life had been spent under the rule of Queen Elizabeth I, a formidable Queen who never married and who therefore had no children to pass on the Crown.

This was a problem throughout her reign. Much of the first part of her time as Queen was spent defending herself against a number of attempts to take the Crown away from her. There was much spying going on, and no one seemed to trust anyone.

One of the biggest threats to the Crown was Mary, Queen of Scots. Queen from only six days old, Mary spent her early years in the French court and married Francis I of France aged 16. Renowned for her beauty, she became Queen of both Scotland and France and was seen as a threat to Elizabeth as she followed the Catholic Church, from which Elizabeth's father King Henry VIII had broken to form the Church of England.

Church of England and Catholicism: what's the difference?

Whilst both are Christian faiths, there are many differences between the **Church of England** (CofE) and the **Catholic Church**.

Mainly, they revolve around who has the final say about how the Christian faith should be explained to the people and how people should express their belief in God.

With **Catholicism** (the oldest of the two faiths), the Pope and his Priests have the last word with all things God related. The Pope has a direct line to God, and no one else. He is 'God's representative on earth'.

The **Church of England** has its roots in **Protestantism** (first seen in 1517 in Germany), although it still upholds some of the customs of the Catholic church. Followers do not recognise the Pope as the keeper of God's word. They believe that the bible speaks directly to them. They do not need someone in Rome to tell them how or what to believe.

As you can imagine, in the 16th Century the newly formed Church of England caused quite a stir! The Roman Catholic church was by far and away the most powerful organisation on earth, and didn't appreciate Henry deciding England no longer needed the Pope in its life. What really rubbed salt into the wound was that Henry decreed he was now God's representative on earth, not the Pope.

Now you can see why things were so turbulent during Shakespeare's life.

As Queen, Elizabeth carried on the Church of England, but Mary wanted to revert to Catholicism, which she called the only true faith.

This left the country divided and deeply afraid, and made Elizabeth rather paranoid (and rightly so).

Elizabeth died in 1603, and James VI of Scotland succeeded in her place. However, many weren't too happy with him, accusing him of being a weak man who was too close to the Catholic church.

Things reached crisis when the Gunpowder Plot of 1605 sought to blow up the Houses of Parliament. We still celebrate this on November 5th. Guy Fawkes and his crew of Catholic rebels attempted to destroy Parliament during its state opening.

They were foiled and put to death in rather a nasty way (check out what it means to be hanged, drawn and quartered).

All this is important when you come to study *Macbeth*. Because even though the storyline was 'borrowed' from Holinshead's *Chronicles* (a history book of the time), and was very loosely based on the 11th Century King of the same name, the themes and ideas explored by the play are highly contemporary (in other words, they very much reflect the time Shakespeare was writing the play).

A King who many believe does not deserve to be on the throne? Plots to remove him? Spying, corruption and paranoia? Yes, all of this was evident during the years Shakespeare was writing and performing and all are certainly evident in the play.

WILLIAM SHAKESPEARE

I won't go into huge detail about the man, as you can find all this out online. However, having a bit of colour is always helpful.

Shakespeare was born in 1564 and baptised on 26 April of that year. Most attribute his birth to the 23rd April which is St George's day, mainly because he died on the same day in 1616. Quite poetic I suppose. But the truth is no one knows exactly what date he was born.

After attending grammar school in Stratford, in 1582 he married Anne Hathaway: he was 18, she was 26. The marriage was arranged quickly, and some six months later Anne gave birth to a daughter, Susanna. No prizes for working out why they were married so quickly.

Two years later, Anne gave birth to twins, Hamnet and Judith. Hamnet died of unknown causes at the age of 11, a death that was to haunt Shakespeare for the rest of his life and one possible reason for Shakespeare giving the play Hamlet its title.

In 1585, Shakespeare went off the map, and didn't appear again until 1592, when he had moved to London. We refer to those years as his 'lost years': there are a few ideas as to what he might have got up to but no one knows for sure.

By 1592, several of Shakespeare's plays were being peformed in London, by 1594 a company of actors called the Lord Chamberlain's Men were performing his plays, and in 1599 several of these men built the Globe Theate on London's South Bank.

You can see a replica of this playhouse on the site of the original, and can even go to watch plays there, in the open air.

During this time Shakespeare became quite wealthy, largely through investing in property. He continued to act throughout his writing career, performing in his and other playwrights' plays.

Like much of his life, the circumstances of Shakespeare's death remain unclear. What we do know is that in his will he bequeathed his 'second best bed' to his wife Anne, which suggests they hadn't been getting on so well in his later years. Again, no one knows.

Shakespeare is buried in the Holy Trinity church in Stratford - you can visit his grave.

The first published full edition of Shakespeare's plays is the First Folio of 1623. There are around 235 copies left in existence - five of them are held by the British Library.

SCENE BY SCENE ANALYSIS

SUMMARY OF THE PLAY

The play is broken into five Acts. This is fairly typical of plays at the time, and follows a structure that has been around ever since writers have been dreaming up stories (more on that later). At its most brief, the play can be summarised thus:

ACT 1

Macbeth returns from battle having proven his bravery. He is given the title of Thane of Cawdor, but his wife Lady Macbeth thinks he deserves more. They plan to murder King Duncan when he comes to visit their castle.

After having second thoughts that are firmly squashed by Lady Macbeth, Macbeth goes ahead with the deed, stabbing King Duncan to death and making it look like it was his servants.

ACT 2

King Duncan is discovered murdered. Macbeth goes to Duncan's bedchamber and kills the servants, seemingly in a fit of passionate revenge. Duncan's two sons, Malcolm and Donalbain, flee the country in fear of their life.

ACT 3

Macbeth is crowned King of Scotland, but Banquo starts to have suspicions about the real reason for Duncan's death. Macbeth realises he will have to murder Banquo, his close friend, if he is remain King.

Banquo is murdered but his son Fleance escapes. At a feast in honour of his coronation, Macbeth sees Banquo's ghost. Lady Macbeth asks the attendees of the feast to leave.

ACT 4

Macbeth goes to see the three Witches to ask them about his future. He wants to know if anyone will threaten his position as King. They tell him to fear Macduff, the Thane of Fife but also that no one who has been born 'of a woman' will defeat him.

He should also not be worried unless Birnam Wood comes to his castle as he believes none of these things can happen.

This gives him confidence. In order to make sure none of Macduff's family can cause him problems in future, Macbeth has Lady Macduff and her children murdered. Macduff hears the news and vows revenge.

ACT 5

Lady Macbeth appears to have lost her mind as the guilt and trauma has become too much for her. She sleepwalks, admitting to having committed terrible acts.

Macbeth waits for the arrival of Macduff but is not concerned as he has been told by the witches that only someone not born by a woman can harm him.

He hears that Lady Macbeth has killed herself by jumping from a window and questions the meaning and worth of life.

Macduff's army approaches Macbeth's castle under cover, by using the branches of the trees from Birnam Wood. He then tells Macbeth that he was not born, but rather was ripped from his mother's womb (through what we would now call caesarian section).

They fight, and Macduff chops off Macbeth's head. Malcolm is made King.

ACT 1

ACT 1 SCENE 1

One of the most famous openings of any play ever written, we join the three Witches as they wait for Macbeth's arrival.

The correct name for the Witches is in fact 'Weird Sisters'. In the original text they were referred to as 'Wayward Sisters'.

It's tempting to think of the Witches like those from the Wizard of Oz, Room on the Broom etc. You know, big noses, warts and broomsticks.

But these witches are more closely aligned with the Three Fates of classical mythology. Indeed, the original spelling of 'Weird' ('Wyrd') actually means 'fate'. The Fates assigned destinies at birth: in other words, they decided what was going to happen to you in future.

The witches don't really cast a spell over Macbeth. They don't do anything particularly magical (other than call up some spirits). What they do is prophecy a future for him, and it's up to Macbeth to follow this. They tell him his fate.

The play begins with 'thunder and lightning'. This is a good example of what is sometimes incorrectly referred to as the *pathetic fallacy*: it is more accurately described as the *objective correlative*.

In a nutshell, the objective correlative is the exterior, natural world reflecting the interior, emotional world of the characters (the objective world correlating (matching) with what's going on inside).

You see, we can't get inside the head of a character in a play in the same way we can in a novel, so a playwright has to use other techniques to show how characters are feeling or to set the mood for the scene.

An example might be the wind blowing when a character is in turmoil, or birds singing when characters fall in love.

We know that *Macbeth* will be a play filled with dark drama, with minds clouded by greed and revenge and emotions churning like a stormy sea. It makes sense to start with a bit of thunder and lightning, don't you think?

In response to the First Witch asking 'When shall we three meet again?', the Second Witch replies 'When the hurly burly's done, when the battle's lost and won.'

This is the first example of a play filled with oxymorons (contradictory phrases, in this case 'lost and won').

These contradictions conclude the short opening scene, with the well-known chant 'fair is foul and foul is fair'. We'll say a lot more about these contradictions/paradoxes in the Themes section.

The Witches set the scene for a play which turns expectations on their head, where the good are murdered and the guilty crowned. Where nothing is as it seems and no one can be trusted. Where appearances are very different from the dark reality underneath.

ACT 1 SCENE 2

We join King Duncan as he questions a wounded Captain who has just returned from battle against the Norwegians.

The Captain explains that Macdonwald (a traitor to the King) was too weak for Macbeth, who confronted him on the battlefield and 'unseamed him from the knave to th' chops' - cut him open from his belly to his throat.

This immediately paints the picture of a man who is fierce and brave in battle and who is loyal to the King. Anyone who can cut a man open like this must be pretty strong.

This is important when we see Macbeth later in the play: here is a man who is excellent in battle but who might not be quite so good at ruling.

The Captain continues, telling King Duncan that the Norwegians had increased their attack but Macbeth and Banquo had faced this attack bravely: 'they doubly redoubled strokes upon the foe'.

The Thane of Ross then arrives, and tells the King that the Norwegians have been defeated and the Thane of Cawdor, another traitor, has been captured.

Duncan announces that Cawdor will be executed and that Macbeth will take his title.

The scene ends with Duncan saying, 'What he hath lost, noble Macbeth hath won.' Notice it's a repetition of the witches' 'lost and won' in Scene 1? That's no accident.

Let's take a moment to explore this key theme of the play.

Binary oppositions

The play is full of binary oppositions. Fair and foul. Dark and light. Male and female. All of these are binaries, so called because of the binary mathematical code (made up of ones and zeros).

The reason this is important is because you can't have one binary without the other - they are two sides of the same coin.

You can't have daytime unless you have night. You can't have a winner unless someone else is a loser.

You can't know goodness unless you compare it to evil. Binaries are fundamental to how we know the world, and plays like Macbeth explore them skilfully.

However, they also raise some interesting questions. The Thane of Cawdor was a traitor to the King, but to the Norwegians would have been seen as a noble rebel.

And Macbeth, a hero to Duncan ,would have been a villain to Macdonwald. You see, nothing is as simple as we might imagine as binaries are often subjective.

ACT 1 SCENE 3

We rejoin the Three Witches as they wait for Macbeth returning home from battle. While they wait, the First Witch tells the others that she'd just come from asking a sailor's wife for some chestnuts.

The sailor's wife had basically told her to clear off - 'aroint thee, witch' - so the witch promised to curse the woman's husband who is sailing to Aleppo (in Syria).

The other witches say they'll help her, by giving her 'a wind'. So, because some random woman didn't give one of the witches some chestnuts, her husband will soon be caught in a terrible storm that will go on for days and days. Seems a bit harsh.

But this is the point. These are women who you don't want to mess with, as they have a supernatural power that makes them dangerous. As we mentioned above, they don't actually use this on Macbeth, but we can see here that they seem to have access to powers that are not normal.

Our heroes enter

Macbeth and Banquo enter the scene. Once again, the theme of 'fair and foul' is repeated, Macbeth saying 'So fair and foul a day I have not seen.'

He can sense that there is something strange about the atmosphere but he cannot work out what it is - these oppositions add to the sense of confusion and mystery that surrounds the start of the play.

Remember, Macbeth has not yet heard about Cawdor's capture or him being given the Thane's title.

Banquo sees the witches and is rather taken aback by how they look - he says they 'look not like th' inhabitants o' th' earth'. He questions whether they are women - 'your beards forbid me to interpret / That you are so.'

Gender expectations: fear of witches

At the time the play was written, there were clear expectations placed on men and women - both how they acted, and how they looked.

Men were active, women were passive (note another binary opposition there). Men decided, women followed. Women were not supposed to have their own minds, but rather were expected to be controlled by the men in their lives. (More on this in the Themes section.)

The witches are problematic in this regard, as they are three independent and therefore dangerous women. Banquo highlights their beards in order to make them seem more masculine: they cannot be normal, feminine women if they are not under the control of men.

You may have heard of witch trials - the most famous ones were in Salem in the USA at the end of the 17th Century, but witches were being tried during Shakespeare's time. In fact, the period from 1580 to 1630 was the high point in Europe for trying witches.

We can now look back on this time and realise that these women were not in possession of some evil forces. They were simply women who others did not trust - perhaps unmarried, or outspoken.

Finding a woman guilty of being a witch was a bit like saying she was guilty of being her own person, of having a point of view and therefore somehow upsetting the status quo - the correct order of things.

As we've seen before, Macbeth's witches were originally called Wyrd Sisters. So nothing to do with being a witch. It was perhaps later that they were called witches, as this fits better the idea of independent women who were feared by men.

We'll go into how women are represented a little later, in the Themes section.

The witches then hail Macbeth:

> *All hail, Macbeth! Hail to thee, Thane of Glamis!*
> *All hail, Macbeth! Hail to thee, Thane of Cawdor!*
> *All hail, Macbeth, that shalt be king hereafter!*

Macbeth is currently Thane of Glamis but does not yet know about Cawdor. This then plants a seed in his mind that will grow into something far larger and more dangerous once he's home with his wife.

However, his initial reaction is one of fear, but Banquo asks him why this is: 'why do you start and seem to fear / Things that do sound so fair?' Once again that word 'fair' shows itself: this surely is good news, Banquo seems to be saying.

Banquo can only see the positive in this - surely if these women are predicting Macbeth becoming king it will be down to merit and not because of any terrible plan he might have.

We can perhaps surmise that Macbeth has, before the play begins, considered the kingship. Perhaps he has not spoken openly to his wife, but he has maybe dreamt about becoming king.

The witches could then simply be projecting his inner desires outwardly. Maybe he looks scared because they've made public his very private fantasies. We don't know, but this immediate, nervy reaction suggests a man who has something dark to hide.

Banquo, on the other hand, sees nothing worrying in this. He immediately asks the witches to tell him his future - perhaps he sees these old women as an amusement, not to be taken too seriously: 'If you can look into the seeds of time / And say which grain will grow and which will not...' (line 60).

The metaphor of a seed is an important one as we've just mentioned. Seeds are cast on the ground, and only some of them grow. Every seed has the potential, but not all this potential is realised.

It's the same with the infinite number of possible futures we have in front of us. There will only be one future, but depends on the choices we make today.

Banquo wants to know which of these seeds will grow into his future. And the witches tell him, rather cryptically at that moment, but in terms that will (literally) come to haunt Macbeth later:

> FIRST WITCH: *Lesser than Macbeth and greater.*
> SECOND WITCH: *Not so happy, yet much happier.*
> THIRD WITCH: *Thou shalt get kings, though thou be none.*

There are those oxymorons again: lesser and greater, not happy but much happier and so on. This riddling way of speaking lends the witches a great sense of mystery. They give the end point, the conclusion, but not the means to get there. Banquo's children will be kings? Is this what they mean? Neither man knows but both are filled with intrigue about their future.

Macbeth commands them to speak: 'Tell me more'. He is hungry for more information but they give him none, disappearing 'into the air'.

When they have gone, Banquo questions their sanity: 'have we eaten on the insane root / That takes reason prisoner?' He is probably referring to hemlock or henbane, both poisons that can cause madness.

This idea of madness is an important one that is developed as the play progresses. We will see both Macbeth and Lady Macbeth slowly lose their sanity, as if they have been poisoned by the choices they have made.

The second prophecy comes true

At that moment Ross and Angus enter, to tell the men that ' the King hath happily received... The news of thy success' and has 'bade me, from him, call thee Thane of Cawdor.'

Banquo's immediate response is important here: he says 'What, can the devil speak true?' He immediately sees the witches' prophecy as being bad news, sent from the devil and to be feared.

Macbeth of course remains confused: 'The thane of Cawdor lives: why do you dress me in borrowed robes?' When he is told of Cawdor's treason and impending execution, Macbeth suddenly realises that what the witches has told him is already coming true.

Macbeth's first 'aside'

We then have the first 'aside' in the play. Let's explore this dramatic technique in a little more detail, as it's an important technique Shakespeare uses in his Tragedies.

Macbeth uses asides throughout the play. An aside is the character turning away from the drama and speaking his thoughts to the audience.

Think of it like pressing pause on the scene: the action on stage is paused and the main character shares how he or she is feeling at that precise moment.

It's a clever technique for three reasons: firstly, because it enables Shakespeare to do something that no other playwright had done before with such success - to get right inside a character's head and understand their motivations.

Secondly, because it inevitably makes us take the main character's side, whether we like it or not. By taking us into his world, Macbeth is privileging us with information that none of the other characters have. This puts us at an advantage.

Which brings us on to the third reason why this is such an effective technique: it enables the playwright to play around with *dramatic irony*: when we know more than the characters on stage.

At its most basic, dramatic irony can be seen in pantomimes when children shout 'look behind you!' The drama is in knowing what is going to happen to characters before they do.

Macbeth begins this aside by putting the first two predictions into context:

> *Two truths are told,*
> *As happy prologues to the swelling act*
> *Of the imperial theme.*

In other words, he knew he was Thane of Glamis (truth no.1) and now knows he is Thane of Cawdor (truth no.2). But are these the warm up act for the main event, aka the 'imperial theme' of becoming king?

'Swelling act' is an interesting way of putting it: meaning growing, getting larger. Could he be referring to his ego at this point? To his ambition? Both are possible.

Perhaps the reality of his dream getting closer. Either way he is intrigued by what the witches have told him.

Macbeth's second aside

After thanking Ross and Angus for the news, he offers us a second, longer aside. This one is a little more complex, so don't worry if it doesn't immediately make sense. The asides are often more complex as they offer us an insight into the workings of an ambitious yet tortured mind.

He begins by showing us his confusion - the 'supernatural soliciting' of the witches 'cannot be ill, cannot be good'. He seems caught between acknowledging the 'success' of becoming thane of Cawdor with the 'horrid image' of becoming king 'against the use of nature'.

And why is it against nature? Because he knows what he will have to do in order to become king. The murder of Duncan 'is yet fantastical', but he has already starting thinking about it.

This suggests he's been harbouring ambitions of becoming king for some time: it would seem odd to believe that he had never considered it to this point and all of a sudden is plotting murder just because three old hags had suggested it.

Macbeth's 'fatal flaw' is his huge ambition. Let's think about this for a moment in relation to the play as a typical Tragedy.

The fatal flaw

In Greek tragedy, the hero would have a quality that, when exaggerated, proved to be their downfall. This was known as their *hamartia*, or fatal flaw.

It would appear to be a positive quality, such as confidence or ambition, but as the play progressed became more and more damaging to the hero and those around him or her.

Macbeth's *hamartia* is his ambition and single-minded determination. On the battlefield it proves highly effective, but as soon as he gets into his head the fact that he wants to become king and ensure no one can remove him, this determination and ambition become deeply poisonous.

The thought of murdering Duncan has so disturbed him that the 'function' of being a brave warrior has been 'smothered in surmise': in other words, he is struggling to function normally due to these terrible yet fascinating thoughts.

He then decides that, if he is to become king, it will happen by chance and 'without my stir' - without him doing anything about it.

This is typical of Macbeth at the start of the play - he cannot make up his mind whether to do the deed, and needs his wife to push him on to finish the job and not just talk about it.

Banquo then comments that Macbeth has not yet become used to this new title: these 'strange garments' do not immediately stick (cleave) to him but will take his shape once they are used.

This is a good example of dramatic irony: during this aside, clearly Macbeth's expression has been one of confusion and perhaps even fear.

Banquo has mistaken that for Macbeth not yet feeling comfortable with his new title. But we know that Cawdor is already old news for Macbeth: he has his eyes on a new prize…

Banquo then prompts Macbeth to stop daydreaming - 'We stay upon your leisure' basically means 'erm, we are waiting for you mate?' Macbeth apologises, saying that he was remembering 'things forgotten', and says he will meet them again soon.

Time for him to meet Duncan and hear it from the horse's mouth.

ACT 1 SCENE 4

Remember, at this point Macbeth is very much in favour within Duncan's court. There is no suggestion of anything suspicious about him, and his bravery in battle has made him a favourite of Duncan's.

Before Macbeth's arrival, Malcolm informs his father that the treasonous thane of Cawdor has been executed, but went to his death with nobility and bravery: 'he confess'd his treasons / Implored your highness' pardon and set forth / A deep repentance.'

Another theme of the play is masculine honour: there is a right way and a wrong way to act if you are to be seen as a noble man. Whilst

Cawdor had lived a traitor, he died nobly, and has gone up in Duncan's estimation as a result.

Duncan then utters one of his best-known lines: 'there's no art / To find the mind's construction in the face'. What does he mean? That a person's appearance can hide the reality of his true nature.

What the mind is thinking, and how the person acts, can be very different things. Duncan had had 'an absolute trust' in Cawdor and was betrayed by him.

Of course, this is hugely ironic based on the fact that the man he is giving the title of Cawdor to will be Duncan's ultimate betrayer. Just goes to show you can't trust anyone nowadays…

Macbeth arrives

It's great timing that at the moment Duncan mentions appearance and reality, Mac-'I'll smile and then stab you in the back'-beth arrives.

Duncan thanks Macbeth for his efforts, telling him that he wished Macbeth had done less so that the reward could have matched the deed: 'the proportion of thanks and payment' are not even in Duncan's eyes.

Macbeth gives a good (if slightly smarmy) reply, telling Duncan that the loyalty he owes is payment enough. There is further irony when he says that the king's subjects should do 'every thing / Safe toward your love and honour'. Of course, Macbeth is thinking of doing the least safe thing possible, i.e. murdering him.

At line 39 Duncan drops his bombshell: he has made Malcolm 'Prince of Cumberland', and in so doing guaranteed that he will be the next king. Macbeth immediately gives us his aside:

> *The Prince of Cumberland! That is a step*
> *On which I must fall down, or else o'erleap,*
> *For in my way it lies.*

The 'let's just see what happens' approach didn't last for long, did it? Of course not - Macbeth would have been happy to let nature take its course provided it ended in him becoming king. Now that Duncan has named his successor he is back to plotting once more.

The appearance and reality theme is repeated at the end of the scene: 'stars hide your fires / Let not light see my black and deep desires.' He doesn't want anyone seeing in his expression that he has dark plans to murder his way into power.

ACT 1 SCENE 5

There's a saying - 'behind every successful man lies a strong woman' (not sure who said it first). This is certainly the case with the Macbeths.

From the moment we meet Lady Macbeth we see a woman whose love of her husband is only matched by her utter determination to ensure he gets what she believes is rightly his. Or is her desire for power more important than her love for Macbeth? It's hard to say.

She enters reading the letter from Macbeth, which explains to her what has just happened - he met the witches, they told him his future, then one part of it immediately came true.

Her first thoughts turn to his character. She believes he is 'too full o' the milk of human kindness' to go through with the murder. And we're thinking: really? He's just sliced someone open and chopped off his head and he's too full of kindness?

This shows the sort of woman Lady Macbeth is. Remember what we said earlier about how women at that time should be submissive, not question or challenge the men in their lives? Well, from the very opening of the play we have a woman who is questioning her husband's courage.

And we would be right in thinking, 'this probably won't end well.' Because, in Shakespeare's Tragedies, any woman who steps outside of what is expected of her tends to meet with a rather bad ending (usually a combination of madness and/or death).

Interestingly, wayward women tend to end up married at the end of his Comedies. Either way they've been tamed.

But I digress (slightly). What we see here, from the very moment Lady Macbeth enters the stage, is a woman with huge ambition and a dark, brutal streak.

Macbeth needs some madness in him

I think what she says next is really interesting:

> *...thou wouldst be great;*
> *Art not without ambition, but without*
> *The illness should attend it.*

What does she mean by this? The first part is pretty simple: Macbeth has ambition (we've certainly seen that) but he lacks the ruthlessness that he needs in order to follow through.

But why 'illness'? Seems an odd word to use. She seems to be suggesting that Macbeth will need some madness in him in order to achieve this goal. That rising to the very top cannot be done if you are entirely sane.

It is an interesting point of view, and one that we cannot help but think is Shakespeare commenting on those in power: that a 'normal', rational person could not be a ruler. You have to be able to make some terrible choices if you want to get, and keep, ultimate power.

Anyone who has seen *House of Cards* on Netflix will know just what I mean. (And if you haven't I really recommend it as part of your revision, as it is Macbeth for a modern age.)

She continues on in the same way (she really doesn't think he has the cojones to do this, does she?) - 'what thou wouldst highly / That wouldst thou holily'. You want the highest honour but you'd only be prepared to do it in a holy, sinless way.

From line 26 she shifts her focus onto herself. She wants him to come to her ('hie thee hither') so she can 'pour my spirits in thine ear / And chastise with the valour of my tongue / All that impedes thee from the golden round.'

It's an interesting metaphor to use: to pour her spirits. It's as if she wants to fill Macbeth with her evil, her dark madness. It sounds like an incantation - almost as if she's a fourth witch.

The second line here is important, as it points to Lady Macbeth's strength and 'valour': she is able to speak courageously and will remove anything that 'impedes' (stops) Macbeth from the 'golden round', or crown.

The 'unsex me here' soliloquy

When a messenger announces that Duncan is on his way to their castle, we have what is one of the most brutally brilliant soliloquies in all of Shakespeare.

A soliloquy is a dramatic technique that has the main character on stage speaking their thoughts to the audience. Often asides take the form of soliloquies, but often they are the character alone on stage. Hamlet's 'To be or not to be' soliloquy is probably the most famous in all literature.

Like an aside, they are designed to allow the audience into the character's mind. They are usually extended, and come at key moments in the play, often before big decisions are made. You'll see several in Macbeth.

Let's remind ourselves of what we explored earlier. At the time the play was written (and indeed up until very recently), women had a certain set of expectations placed upon them. There were certain things you just did not do if you were a woman. Speaking your mind, having strong opinions, being argumentative, assertive, and so on.

You were under the control of your father until you were married, then 'given away' to the husband through the marriage ceremony. Do you think marriage is an institution that was created to enable two people to publicly declare their love for one another?

Think again: it was a legal act of transference of ownership. It may have a different purpose now, but more traditionally it was a far more functional act.

The reason this is important in the context of the play is that, in order for Lady Macbeth to give her husband the courage he needs to commit regicide (the murder of a king), she needs to strip away anything female from her body and mind.

This clearly shows us that these female qualities were seen as negative when it came to anything to do with power. Being female was a sign of weakness, and Lady Macbeth cannot afford to be weak at this moment.

She begins with these powerful words:

> …*Come, you spirits*
> *That tend on mortal thoughts, unsex me here*
> *And fill me from the crown to the toe top-full*
> *Of direst cruelty!*

She commands the supernatural world to enter her and remove her femininity, to fill her with evil so that she can share some of this with Macbeth. She knows he lacks it, and it would appear she lacks it herself.

If she needs to summon courage in order to go through with the act, does this suggest she is also not strong enough? Remember that this is a man writing about a woman: the comment being made her seems to be that she has to remove anything female in order to be strong enough.

We will see that blood is an important *motif* in the play. A motif is an image which is repeated and links to a theme. By saying 'make thick my blood' she is asking these spirits to give her both strength and to remove compassion.

Blood is the life force, so by thickening it she is almost suggesting she becomes less alive, less human.

Notice also the sounds of the language throughout this soliloquy. 'Make thick' almost sounds onomatopoeic: the repeated 'k' slows the reading down as the thickened blood would slow.

It's important with a play like Macbeth that you focus on the poetry of the language: this will help move your grade up towards the 8 and 9.

We then have another brutal image, as she commands these spirits ('murdering ministers') to 'come to my women's breasts / And take my milk for gall.' Gall is the bile obtained from an animal and used in medicine. It is a very bitter substance: we use the word now to mean an act that leaves a bitter taste in the mouth.

What is important here is that she is referring to the very substance that gives life to a baby, her mother's milk, wanting to turn it into something bitter and unpalatable. She is prepared to remove anything comforting or life-giving from her body as this is the only way she can achieve her goal.

The final words of this disturbing incantation command the spirits to cover her in the 'smoke of hell' so that the knife does not see the 'wound it makes' and heaven cannot see what she is doing and tell her to stop ('hold, hold!').

We do need to put a speech like this into context. No one to this point in the history of literature had so brutally confronted the depths of depravity that people will stoop to in order to achieve their goals.

Shakespeare shows both his genius with language and his understanding of human psychology. This is why you're studying it now! Trust me, learning this stuff pays off in the long run.

I know I may be biased, but every time I read this it gives me chills. It is also exceptional to watch on stage. I urge you to locate a stage version of this and go and see it. Failing that, check out one of the many excellent productions of the play on film. I'll give some recommendations at the end of this book.

Macbeth arrives

Showing perfect timing, Macbeth returns home. The poetic, spell-like language of previous is replaced by cold, hard facts. After repeating the witches' hail, Macbeth tells her that Duncan is coming to their castle.

When she asks him when the king will leave, Macbeth replies 'To-morrow, as he purposes.' She responds 'O, never / Shall sun that morrow see!'

And there it is. A decision has been made, with no debate. Lady Macbeth has decided that Duncan will be murdered that night - he will never see the sun again.

Macbeth's expression clearly tells a different story - we know this because Lady Macbeth immediately goes on to say 'Your face…is a book / Where men may read strange matters.' This refers back to Macbeth's earlier aside, where he says 'Let not light see my black and deep desires'.

It also builds on the image of the 'smokes of hell': they have to conceal their intentions from everyone.

This is further developed when Lady Macbeth tells her husband to 'look like the innocent flower / But be the serpent under it.' The serpent is a traditional image of evil - in the Bible, Satan appears as a snake in the Garden of Eden, tempting Eve with an apple and causing her and Adam to fall from grace and be cast out.

Do you think he gets the message? I would hope so.

I quite like Macbeth's short answer: 'We will speak further.' He's not convinced at this stage and I get the impression he doesn't want his wife to keep going on about it. He has heard enough for one day.

I mean, you come home from a hard day's battle, having just chopped a man's head off, and the first thing you hear when you're home is your wife telling you they're going to kill the king that evening? He doesn't even get a chance to make a cup of tea. Poor Macbeth.

Lady Macbeth, however, isn't interested in any reservations. She tells him to 'look up clear': in other words, have a blank, clear expression so that he gives nothing away. As far as she is concerned, the decision has been made.

ACT 1, SCENE 6

The first words of this scene are hugely ironic: we've just heard Lady Macbeth tell her husband that they will murder Duncan that evening, and we immediately cut to Duncan saying 'This castle hath a pleasant seat; the air / Nimbly and sweetly recommends itself / Unto our gentle senses.'

This is an excellent example of dramatic irony: as an audience we are thinking 'you have no idea what a nest of snakes you've just arrived in. Watch yourself!' To Duncan, the castle is pleasant, the air sweet; but we've just had Lady Macbeth command evil spirits to mask her in the 'smokes of hell'. That's quite a contrast.

This is once again an example of the objective correlative: Duncan is in a good mood and the environment around him reflects that mood. We will see a very different description given later by Lennox, in Act 2 Scene 3, after Duncan's murder. For now though, all is calm.

Banquo carries this on, perhaps a little over-the-top. Look at the language he uses: 'summer…loved…heaven's breath…wooed.' We once again see how Shakespeare focuses as much on the sounds of the words as the words themselves. Compare the softness of this speech to Lady Macbeth's earlier and you'll see what I mean.

The dramatic irony continues when Lady Macbeth welcomes Duncan. Whilst on the surface, 'every point twice done and then done double' seems to refer to her making sure everything is perfect for his arrival (check twice and then twice more), this could also refer to his imminent meeting with a pointed dagger.

She says that not even checking this carefully is enough to match the honour of having him in her house: based on what we've just heard, her exaggerated desire to appear the perfect hostess is rather unpleasant to see. We understand at this point just how good she is at being the serpent under the flower.

The scene concludes with Duncan asking Lady Macbeth to take them to Macbeth. He calls Lady Macbeth his 'fair and noble hostess'. There's that word 'fair' again. Only this time, he's miles off the mark. Fair is certainly foul on this occasion.

ACT 1 SCENE 7

Macbeth's first soliloquy

Whilst we've had Macbeth utter a few asides earlier in the play, this is his first proper soliloquy. It comes that evening, before Duncan is murdered, and shows a tortured man unsure as to whether he can go through with the deed.

Remember what I was saying earlier about Shakespeare being the first writer to really get inside a person's head and explore his psychology? This soliloquy is a great example.

In many ways this is one of the most important scenes in the play. It shows that Macbeth still has some free will, some ability to choose good from evil.

Once Duncan is murdered there is no going back, and we no longer hear the contents of his mind until the end of the play: and by then it is too late. It is certainly one of the most powerful scenes in all of Shakespeare.

Let's dive in.

Macbeth starts by repeating 'done' three times. The first two refer to the act being finished; the third refers to it being performed. Macbeth wants it over with quickly - if it has to be done, then let it be done with one 'blow'.

If you struggle a little with these lines don't worry: Macbeth is not in a good place in his head, and the repetition and long, complex phrases show this clearly.

From line 9 we see Macbeth worried about the future: if he murders to become king, he will be setting a dangerous precedent. If one man can become king through murder, then who's to say the same thing won't happen to him?

These 'Bloody instructions' he will be teaching his people could 'return / To plague the inventor': in other words, he could end up murdered in the same way he is considering murdering Duncan. It would be, he ironically says, 'even-handed justice'.

Notice we are already seeing the beginnings of the paranoia that will destroy Macbeth. This is one of the hallmarks of a dictator: they believe everyone is out to remove them from power, and they do all they can to prevent this from happening.

In the lines that follow, Macbeth convinces himself not to go through with it. Duncan is here 'in double trust': Macbeth is both loyal to him as a subject and is also Duncan's host. Macbeth should 'shut the door' against any murderer, 'Not bear the knife myself'.

From lines 16 to 25 we have some pretty dramatic language, all of which is making clear that Duncan is such a good man and excellent king that murdering him would bring 'damnation' on anyone who did so. His death will provoke such 'pity' in the world that 'tears shall drown the wind'.

The image of the 'naked new-born babe' and 'heaven's cherubim' only serve to reinforce Duncan's greatness and innocence. Macbeth paints an almost God-like image of him, which would make his murder a terrible sin.

Before Lady Macbeth's entrance, he has decided:

> ...*I have no spur*
> *To prick the sides of my intent, but only*
> *Vaulting ambition, which oe'rleaps itself*
> *And falls on th'other.*

Macbeth uses the metaphor of a horse-rider: he has no good motive to murder Duncan, only his immense ambition, which, if he is not careful, will take him too far (in the way that a horse rider could vault over the other side of the horse if he propels himself too enthusiastically into the saddle).

Lady Macbeth enters

Macbeth informs his wife immediately that 'We will proceed no further in this business'. Short, sharp and to the point. He's had plenty of time to consider and wants nothing more to do with this dreadful plan.

And what reason does he give? Duncan has recently given him the honour of thane of Cawdor and people are speaking highly of him right now, which he does not want to end.

He wants these compliments to 'be worn now in their newest gloss': to enjoy them as he might a new outfit. Look, you can't blame him for wanting to bask in the glow of being a hero for a little longer, can you?

As you can imagine, Lady Macbeth isn't too pleased about this (understatement of the year). We now see her for who she really is: this is all about her and her desire for power through her husband. She shows little love or care for the man at this point.

She echoes the clothing metaphor Macbeth has just used: 'Was the hope drunk / Wherein you dressed yourself?' Was the hope to be king that you showed me before actually meaningless? She wonders whether he was ever serious about becoming king: she is already doubting his character.

She asks whether this 'hope' has now woken up, hungover (green and pale), looking at the situation very differently. None of you will know this, of course, but when you're drunk you often feel a lot more confident about things than you do the next morning.

There's then a stinging, and in my opinion, rather passive aggressive comment: 'Such I account thy love'. From now on, Lady Macbeth will consider that he loves her in the same way that he has shown desire for the crown - in other words, weakly and without conviction. She is highlighting this weakness, and this is not a good thing for a warrior like Macbeth to hear.

Macbeth wants his fish without getting his feet wet

She then twists the knife some more (pardon the pun):

> *Art thou afeard*
> *To be the same in thine own act and valour*
> *As thou art in desire? Wouldst thou have that*
> *Which thou esteem'st the ornament of life,*
> *And live a coward in thine own esteem,*
> *Letting 'I dare not' wait upon 'I would,'*
> *Like the poor cat I' the adage?*

Are you scared to be as brave in action as you are in words? Are you happy living a coward with these golden opinions others have of you? Would you rather say 'I dare not' than 'I would', like the cat who would eat the fish but not get his feet wet?

Ouch! That has to hurt noble Macbeth. Calling someone like him a coward will sting: he has shown tremendous bravery on the battlefield and everyone thinks he's a hero, but his wife is telling him something very different.

Lady Macbeth appears to be using a technique we'd most likely call 'reverse psychology'. You'll have had it used on you, several times no doubt. 'I don't believe you can eat all your peas,' or 'That maths problem is far too hard for someone of your age to do.' Telling someone they can't do something so that they think 'I'll show you'. It works pretty well with children, so it's interesting that Lady Macbeth is using it on Macbeth.

This approach certainly gets under Macbeth's skin: his response ('Prithee, peace') suggests a man who is not happy with what his wife is saying and wants her to stop. You can almost imagine him putting his hands over his ears and saying 'lalala, not listening' (I haven't seen a version of Macbeth with him doing this, but it would be appropriate I think).

The theme of masculinity (which we'll look at in more detail later) is continued when he says 'I dare do all that may become a man / Who dares do more in none.' I will do what is needed to prove my masculinity. Doing more than this is not manly. In other words, stabbing the king is not the sort of thing real men do.

He has a point: as we will see very soon with he goes through with the murder, there is something deeply cowardly about stabbing someone to death in their sleep.

As we have come to expect, Lady Macbeth has an answer to this, and takes this idea of manliness and turns it on her head. If you do it, then you are so much more a man - because being king is the ultimate in masculine pride.

The most terrible image of all

In line 54, we have one of the most terrible images in all of Shakespeare (and this is from a playwright who, in one of his earlier earlier play, has a woman come on stage with her hands chopped off and tongue cut out so that she cannot point the finger of blame at her rapists (see Shakespeare's play *Titus Andronicus* for more information).

> *I have given suck, and know*
> *How tender 'tis to love the babe that milks me:*
> *I would, while it was smiling in my face,*
> *Have pluck'd my nipple from its boneless gums,*
> *And dash'd its brains out, had I so sworn as you*
> *Have done this.*

Lady Macbeth says she would rather take her baby from her nipple and smash its brains out than admit what Macbeth is admitting now. That's about as ugly an image as you can get, and shows the lengths this woman will go to in order to get what she wants.

What's also interesting here is that she says she has nursed a child in the past. We can guess that her baby died as the Macbeths have no children. Is this what has made her so hard and cold? Not being a mother? Shakespeare seems to be hinting at this.

Remember what we said about women who cannot be trusted? Women without children were often thought of as witches. There appears to be something unnatural about women who don't have children.

Shakespeare doesn't say it out loud, but to the audiences of the time there is a comment here on femininity and motherhood. If a woman is prepared to murder her nursing baby rather than backing out of this murder, there is clearly something wrong with her.

We'll explore ideas of motherhood in a later section, as it's a key theme of the play and an interesting contrast with the masculine theme we've just touched on.

What we can say here is that Lady Macbeth is taking the most precious of all moments of motherhood and tearing it apart. That's how important being queen is to her.

If we fail?

It would appear Macbeth gets the message. Not very subtle so you'd hope so. However, he is still unsure. 'If we should fail?' He says. Lady Macbeth's response is quite straightforward: 'We fail!'.

She's been about as dramatic as she can possible be, so there is little point in overdoing now. However, she does give a final mark of punctuation, by adding 'But screw your courage to the sticking-place / And we'll not fail.'

The image here might link to the screwing of the string to a cross-bow: Lady Macbeth uses language that Macbeth would be able to relate to. It's a pretty masterful display of persuasion when you think about it.

The plan

She then calmly explains the plan to Macbeth. Lines 61-72 clearly show us what they intend to do. When Duncan is asleep, Lady Macbeth will get his servants drunk and entertain them to the extent that they lose their memory: 'memory, the Warder of the brain, / Shall be a fume'. When they are asleep, Macbeth and Lady Macbeth can do what they like to Duncan. They will then pin the blame on the servants.

Cunning? Perhaps. But there is still plenty that can go wrong between the words and the act itself.

Macbeth seems convinced: in fact, it's rather a one-eighty when you think about it. He now seems completely ready to go through with it.

The language of masculinity is once again employed to indicate his readiness: 'Bring forth men-children only... I am settled, and bend up / Each corporal agent to this terrible feat.' I have decided, and every part of my body will be ready to do the job.

The scene ends in typical Shakespearean fashion. Whenever there is an important scene like this, he'll often end with a rhyming couplet. In this case it repeats the earlier theme of appearance and reality:

> *Away, and mock the time with fairest show:*
> *False face must hide what the false heart doth know.*

What's interesting about this is that it's now Macbeth directing his wife: to this point it's been the other way around. Now that Macbeth has made up his mind he is suddenly assertive: he tells Lady Macbeth to leave and to put on a show of being a good hostess - their expressions must hide their true intentions.

Over the next few scenes, through Act 2 and into Act 3, we will see a shift in the power dynamic between Macbeth and his wife (to be blunt, who wears the trousers).

It's one of the most interesting things about the play, and is certainly something that could come up in the exam, as their relationship is a profoundly important part of what follows.

ACT 2

ACT 2 SCENE 1

A change in mood

Shakespeare is a master at playing with the audience's emotions. We've just had an intense scene, with a couple agreeing to regicide. There is huge drama in this, with the audience desperate to see what happens next.

So what does Shakespeare do? He cuts to a quiet scene with Banquo chatting with his son Fleance. It's an effective way to give the audience a short breather before the drama that is to follow.

However, all is not well in Banquo's mind. He senses something wrong: perhaps it is how dark the night is - he mentions that the 'candles' are 'all out' - there are no stars or moonlight. He is tired ('a heavy summons lies like lead upon me') but he is unable to sleep.

It's most likely because of what the witches told him and Macbeth. It has really bothered him, and he hasn't yet had a chance to speak to Macbeth about it. Perhaps having Duncan suddenly here under Macbeth's roof has unnerved Banquo? Whatever the reason, he senses something wrong about the night.

This is another good example of the objective correlative: the darkness of the night mirroring the darkness of the Macbeths's minds. It also links to the idea of hidden reality: it is easy to hide the truth in the dark.

Sure enough, as soon as Macbeth arrives Banquo wants to talk about the witches. He says he has had a dream about them, and that they have 'showed some truth' to Macbeth. Has he seen something in Macbeth's expression previously? Something that has made him question Macbeth's true intentions?

We know that Macbeth is someone who finds it hard to hide his emotions: both Banquo and Lady Macbeth have mentioned this so far. Banquo must have noticed something: either that or he was so spooked by the witches that he cannot get their words out of his head. Perhaps both.

Is this a dagger…

After Banquo and Fleance exit, Macbeth gives us another fantastic soliloquy. In it, he imagines he sees a dagger in front of him, leading him towards Duncan's bedchamber. He speaks to the dagger - 'Come, let me clutch thee'- but is unable to take hold of it.

He calls it a 'fatal vision', meaning 'a vision linked to fate' rather than anything deadly. He believes the dagger is fate telling him that he should go through with the murder. However, he is not sure whether this dagger is real ('sensible') or 'A dagger of the mind' that has come from his 'heat-oppressed brain'.

In truth, Macbeth is hallucinating because his mind is beyond stressed. He is about to commit the worst possible crime, and whilst he ended the previous scene full of confidence, there seems to be a huge part of his subconscious that totally rejects what he is about to do.

The dagger changes, becoming covered in 'gouts of blood': Macbeth knows that this blood is there because of the impending murder. We will see later how blood symbolises guilt: both Macbeth and Lady Macbeth are haunted by blood on their hands that they cannot seem to remove.

From line 49 we have a series of dark images linked to night:

> *Now o'er the one halfworld*
> *Nature seems dead, and wicked dreams abuse*
> *The curtained sleep; witchcraft celebrates*
> *Pale Hecate's offerings…'*

To Macbeth, the night brings with it the darker side of humanity - witchcraft and evil dreams. Hecate is the goddess of witchcraft, the Three Witches' ruler.

He seems to be calling up those same evil spirits that we have just seen Lady Macbeth summoning: whilst less of an incantation, by acknowledging the presence of these spirits he recognises their importance as he prepares to commit murder.

Notice how Macbeth personifies murder as 'wither'd', who moves 'with his stealthy pace…towards his design'. In this case his 'design' is the murder of Duncan.

Macbeth makes it sound like it is murder itself creeping towards Duncan's bedchamber, not himself. Is he trying to remove himself a little from what is about to happen?

This is a difficult passage, and for a reason. As we've just mentioned, Macbeth is in the midst of mental anguish, and the dark and disjointed images point to the contents of his mind.

From line 56 the tone changes a little. Macbeth asks the earth to 'hear not my steps', because he does not want the stones to 'prate of my whereabout' - speak about his current location. If they do, they will 'take the present horror from the time' - in other words, stop him from committing the act in the dead of night, when it is best done.

Just before the rings he ends with a rhyming couplet - he reminds himself that the longer he talks 'threat', Duncan 'lives'.

He needs to get on with it. He also realises that the longer he talks, the less he wants to go through with it: these words give 'cold breath' to the 'heat of deeds' - pour cold water on his intentions.

The bell rings, and Macbeth leaves to murder the king. Notice that final binary opposition - heaven and hell? Once again this shows Macbeth's tortured, conflicted mind.

This is where the fun really starts! Unless you're Duncan, of course. Or one of his servants. Or Banquo, for that matter.

ACT 2 SCENE 2

Lady Macbeth enters, having fulfilled her side of the bargain by getting Duncan's servants drunk. She seems filled with confidence ('That which hath made them drunk hath made me bold'), but we see this is an illusion when she is suddenly startled by the shriek of an owl.

In truth, she may have been all 'be a man and do the deed' to Macbeth earlier that night, but she is just as terrified as he is. She knows that they have committed treason, and will be put to death if the truth comes out.

She refers to the owl as a 'fatal bellman'. This is because, in Shakespeare's time, an owl flying over a house was seen as an evil omen, signalling the death of someone inside.

A bellman would ring the 'passing bell' when someone was near death, to encourage those in the village to pray for that person. She already seems paranoid, fearful that the owl will give away what has just been done.

She explains that she has 'drugged' the 'possets' of the grooms - plied their drink with a sedative so that they sleep through the murder.

Macbeth then calls out, but Lady Macbeth doesn't initially recognise his voice: remember, it's very dark, so she cannot see her husband.

Her thoughts immediately leap to the plan having failed - 'Alack, I am afraid they have awaked / And 'tis not done.' She immediately blames Macbeth for this, saying that 'he could not miss' the daggers she had laid out for him.

What is interesting is the last thing she says - 'Had he not resembled / My father as he slept, I had done't.' She would have gone through with the murder herself if Duncan had not looked like her father.

Is she making excuses her for why she made her husband do it? Trying to make herself believe that she had the nerve to commit regicide? Probably both. But we already begin to see a woman lying to herself, which will only increase as the charade of their reign begins.

What then follows is a wonderful example of how to create drama through dialogue. Notice how quickfire it is - they are both so wound up that their speech has become staccato. The combination of not being able to see, plus the terrible thing they have jointly done, has put them both on the edge of their nerves.

Why doesn't the murder happen on stage?

You may be wondering why Shakespeare does not show Duncan's murder. After all, we see Banquo's and Macduff's son's murder. What this is an example of is an 'off scene' event: Shakespeare probably does this so that we retain a little sympathy for Macbeth.

We have seen how the witches have planted the seed in his mind, and how that seed has been well watered by his wife. Shakespeare is suggesting that Macbeth isn't entirely responsible for Duncan's death, and by keeping it off scene he is able to keep a little sympathy for the man.

It makes sense: seeing Macbeth stabbing a nice old man is not a good look, and the other murders are committed by hired killers, not by Macbeth himself.

By the way, the word 'obscene' comes from this idea of things that are too horrible for the audience to see being off scene. Not the first word that has its origins in Shakespeare.

Blood on his hands

Lady Macbeth regains her composure a little when Macbeth looks at his bloody hands and says 'this is a sorry sight'. Her response - 'A foolish thing to say a sorry sight' - is a good example of how she continually puts Macbeth back on track during the first part of the play.

She cannot have him showing any regret now - she needs him to remain strong and focused.

Macbeth then recounts the events of the murder. He seems fixated on the servants - one of them laughed in his sleep and one cried 'murder' - it appears that Duncan's murder woke them up.

However, they seemed to say their prayers before falling back to sleep. Perhaps Lady Macbeth didn't drug them enough, or perhaps Duncan's cries woke them? Macbeth does not say.

He seems to be ranting now, like a madman. He wonders why he could not say 'Amen' when one of the servants said 'God bless us!'. Why is this important to him? In truth, it is of no importance: Macbeth is fixating on small, meaningless details because his nerves are shot to pieces.

Lady Macbeth can see this, and tries to calm him: 'Consider it not so deeply…These deeds must not be thought / After these ways; so, it will make us mad.'

She needs Macbeth to stop going over the details - they need to clear the evidence (aka the blood all over his hands and the daggers) and leave the scene. Frankly, Macbeth needs to snap out of it. Time is running out and the body will soon be discovered…

Sleep no more

There then follows one of the most important motifs in the play. Remember the motif? It's a recurring image, one that, as it builds throughout the play, becomes a major theme.

Macbeth is sure he hears a voice cry 'Sleep no more! / Macbeth does murder sleep.' There's a quite lovely bit of poetry that follows, where he describes sleep as

> *The death of each day's life, sore labour's bath,*
> *Balm of hurt minds, great nature's second course,*
> *Chief nourisher in life's feast.*

Why does talk about sleep so much at this point in the play? We'll see as the play develops, as with the murder of Duncan goes any chance of peace for either character again. Macbeth seems almost wistful when he talks about sleep here - it's actually one of the very few positive-sounding images in the entire play.

This is one of the things I love about Shakespeare: we can be in the middle of absolute trauma and he can still stop and deliver us the most exquisite poetry. Clever chap.

Lady Macbeth doesn't appreciate this short poetic interlude however: we can hear the irritation in her voice when she says 'What do you mean?' In other words - *what are you going on about?*

She tries to keep herself calm (someone has to after all). She tells him that all this obsessive thinking will make him weak - will 'unbend your noble strength'.

Man up, Macbeth

However, when she sees the dagger in his hands, and he refuses to take them back to the bedchamber, she loses her temper. 'Infirm of purpose!' she says to him. She cannot believe that he has failed to do such an important thing, and doesn't have the courage to go back in and sort out his mess.

She takes the daggers, telling him that 'the sleeping and the dead / Are but as pictures: 'tis the eye of childhood / That fears a painted devil.' There is no danger in the bedchamber - both Duncan and the sleeping servants are like pictures - and only children are terrified of scary pictures.

Blood as guilt

We are reminded of just how tense Macbeth is when a knocking makes him almost jump out of his skin. 'Why is it that every noise appals me?' he says. Doesn't take a genius to work that one out, Macbeth.

He then looks at his hands, and we get another important motif: the hands that will never be clean. He believes that no sea will ever get his hands clean again - rather, it will turn the 'multitudinous seas incarnadine / Making the green one red.'

Blood is a metaphor for guilt, and this guilt will (as we have mentioned) come to haunt the couple until the end of their lives.

Which, as we know, aren't particularly long lives from this point.

Lady Macbeth returns, covered in blood and ashamed of her husband's cowardice. 'My hands are of your colour / But I shame to wear a heart so white.'

I guess she must have thought that, as a brave warrior, Macbeth would have no problem with killing another man. After all, he'd done enough killing on the battlefield.

What she hadn't considered was Macbeth's fundamental honour: serving the king was an intrinsic part of the male honour code, and committing regicide is in many ways the very worst thing an honourable man can do.

He has allowed himself to be overcome with greed and has been almost bullied into the act by his wife.

Now, I'm not for one moment saying we should feel sorry for Macbeth at this point in the play. However, Shakespeare is not making it easy for us here (when does he ever?).

There is a degree of ambiguity in the presentation of Macbeth's character at this point. Whereas Lady Macbeth has changed little since making up her mind to kill Duncan, Macbeth has journeyed through a number of profound emotions, and is now at his wit's end.

Of course, we will soon see another side to Macbeth, but at this point in the play he seems vulnerable and weak, and we probably do feel more sympathy for him than his wife.

A little water clears us of this deed

There is a bucketload of irony when Lady Macbeth says 'a little water clears us of this deed: / How easy 'tis, then!' This stressing of how simple it is to wash the blood from their hands and therefore remove any trace of their role in the murder does of course indicate to us that Lady Macbeth probably doesn't believe that herself. It's as if she's saying *Don't worry, everything will be fine, just need to wash our hands!*

If only it were that easy… It will take a little more than a bit of soap to clear them of what they've done. But she has to get Macbeth out of that place because clearly someone is on their way. It's almost as if she is talking to a hysterical child.

The last words of Macbeth clearly show us his regret: he wishes the knocking could wake Duncan, and he also wishes he did not know himself because of what he has done.

Too late, Macbeth. You're all in now. No turning back!

ACT 2 SCENE 3

Some comic relief

After the drama, the audience needs a breather. This is where comic relief comes in (no, I don't mean the annual TV comedy show that raises money for charity). The Porter has been placed in the play for one main reason: to offer the audience a bit of a laugh after the torturous previous scene.

This is a pretty typical convention - we see it all the time in the movies. Next time you watch a horror movie or a tense thriller, look at how the scenes are paced. It's likely that a really gory or terrifying scene is followed by a calmer scene: this is because we need these opportunities to catch our breath. Films who don't offer these risk losing their audience - banging your head against a wall without stopping kind of hurts after a while.

So, the Porter's role here is largely to give us all a rest. What we shouldn't be surprised about is that he also comments quite perceptively on some of the key themes of the play. In this respect he plays the role of 'courtly fool' or 'jester': a conventional character in the Tragedy genre, and one seen in the majority of Shakespeare's plays.

The courtly fool

These characters traditionally take two forms: either a clown, used to provide pure entertainment to the audience, or the jester, whose dark humour comments on the action of the play whilst seemingly doing to in a humorous way. Clowns had been around a long time before Shakespeare, but the courtly fool/jester was a more recent Elizabethan invention.

In essence, the role of the courtly fool is to act as the outsider, commenting on the action without fear of punishment.

It is precisely because they sit outside the bounds of normal, civil society that they are able to do this. They are not seen as a threat - indeed, they are welcomed by those in power, as they will speak the truth and not just say what the king or queen might want to hear.

As well as *Macbeth*, we see them in many other Shakespeare plays: *A Midsummer Night's Dream* (Bottom), *The Tempest* (Trinculo), *The Merchant of Venice* (Gobbo), *Twelfth Night* (Feste), and *As You Like It* (Touchstone).

They are often unpleasant-looking or seeming characters at first glance, and are often despised by the other characters. But as the audience we often warm to them or feel some sympathy because of their outcast status.

These are clever men, with a sharp wit and the ability to see through the lies and politics, and offer the audience the raw truth. Let's look at how the Porter fits into this role.

His function is a little different from other courtly fools, as he is not part of any direct action, only making an appearance now. But his role is no less important because of this.

What you'll straight away is that the Porter speaks in prose, not poetry. We haven't looked at this in any detail yet - we'll do so later in this guide.

In brief, if you look back at the previous scene, you'll notice that the Macbeths are speaking in what we call blank verse - (largely) unrhyming lines of ten syllables (known as pentameter as there are five beats in each line).

This is a conventional drama form at the time - Shakespeare didn't invent this. Of course, not every line has five beats - shorter lines won't, for example. But compare the opening of the last scene with the opening of this one:

> *That which hath made them drunk hath made me bold;*
> *What hath quenched them hath given me fire.*

You can hear the rhythm of the above, with stresses on 'That….made…drunk….made….bold.' However, when we listen to the Porter we hear something very different:

> *Here's a knocking indeed! If a man were a porter of hell-gate,*
> *he should have old turning the key.*

There's no line break, no real rhythm to this. It's far more conventionally reported speech, more colloquial and natural sounding. So why does Shakespeare do this?

It's pretty simple: important people get to speak poetry, and the commoners, like porters and servants and murderers, are only allowed to speak prose. It's a way of Shakespeare saying that the former have higher status, possess more intellect, have more ability to present complex emotions and motivations.

The Porter's opening words

It's safe to say that the humorous references the Porter makes at the beginning are pretty lost on us as a modern audience, as many of them are topical - in other words, are relevant to the audience at the time the play was written.

The Porter imagines what it would be like to be the porter of hell: who would he welcome in? First of all a farmer, who had hoarded his crops in the expectation of being able to sell them for inflated prices during the next famine - but the famine never comes so he hangs himself.

Second in line to be welcomed into hell is who the Porter refers to as 'the great equivocator'. Let's take a moment's aside to consider who this person was, as the events to which the porter is alluding are significant in the life of Shakespeare himself.

The Gunpowder Plot

As we mentioned earlier, a lot was going on during the period in which Shakespeare was active as a playwright and actor. One of the most significant events, at around the time Macbeth was first performed, was the Gunpowder Plot.

This concerned a small group of Catholics who were fed-up with being persecuted by the ruling Protestant monarchy and government, who planned to blow up the British parliament and King James.

Luckily for the King, only moments before the explosion was due to be set off, a letter surfaced which warned him of the imminent attack. James had the palace searched, and Guy Fawkes was discovered, match in hand, about to set light to barrels of gunpowder.

As we all know, this was on November 5th: which is why we have fireworks on this date and still burn 'Guys' on a bonfire.

The conspirators were all executed in the most unpleasant fashion, and because Shakespeare knew these men - his father and the chief conspirator's father were close friends - suspicion naturally fell on Shakespeare.

Writing Macbeth, with its clear message that conspirators will end up punished and presenting Duncan as a noble, good Scottish king, cleared Shakespeare of any potential link with the conspirators, as it was clear to King James that Shakespeare was loyal to him.

The Great Equivocator, as the Porter mentions, was actually a Jesuit priest by the name of Father Henry Garnet. He initially denied any knowledge of the plot, but when he was found to be lying he said that God told him to do it. An equivocator is someone who uses ambiguous (vague) language in order to hide the truth.

He was hanged, as you can imagine.

Third is a tailor who tries to cut costs by reducing the amount of fabric in his garments - only he is found out when tighter-fitting French garments become impossible to wear (I know, not funny to us, but you have to assume this would be humorous to the audience at the time).

As I mention above, all of these references are designed to give the audience a bit of a laugh, and also of course enable Macbeth and his wife to leave the stage and get cleaned up - so a pause between action.

And why is this little speech by the Porter important? Because it centres around men who, in their desire to

Drink, the great equivocator

On Macduff and Lennox's arrival (they were the ones knocking as they've just arrived to see the king), the Porter admits that he is still drunk, and explains to Macduff the advantages and disadvantages of alcohol.

57

He says it provokes three things - 'sleep, nose-painting, and urine'. As you can see, these are very different subjects to the grand, ambitious and frankly rather evil topics that have been under discussion thus far in the play.

He then goes on to explain that alcohol is an 'equivocator', as it arouses a man but makes him unable to get an erection ('makes him stand to, and not stand to').

It's all pretty basic, but would have got the audience rolling the aisles. Indeed, there are some modern film versions of this that are quite funny as it lends itself well to visual humour. See the end for suggested movies worth watching.

Whilst it may seem that this has nothing to do with the key themes of the play, of course it does - because nothing in Shakespeare is redundant or accidental.

Macbeth is also something of an equivocator - wanting the crown but not the terrible things that have to be done in order to achieve and maintain this, being both brave warrior and coward, and so on. He also hides behind language, as we will see later in the play.

Macbeth enters

This is the first big test for Macbeth: he has to meet with Macduff and keep a straight face. He cannot give anything away about the crime he has just committed. Notice how short Macbeth keeps his replies to Macduff - the less he says, the better.

Lennox comments on how stormy the night has been, using highly poetic language. Chimneys blown down, 'strange screams of death', 'dire combustion and confused events': it is as if nature itself knew that something terrible was happening.

This is significant: the king was seen as having a direct line in to God. King Henry VIII (he of the six wives and Queen Elizabeth I's father) had broken off England's relationship with the Catholic church of Rome and had founded a new faith, the Church of England. In this new faith, there was no one in between the King and God - the King was God's representative on earth, not the Pope.

This is why the Catholic and Protestant (Church of England) faiths have been at war with each other ever since. Both believe they have the direct line in to the Almighty.

To murder the king was to upset the very order of the natural world: it doesn't get much worse than killing God's right hand man. This is why nature seems to be rebelling at the very moment Duncan is murdered.

All good propaganda for Shakespeare, and certainly got him off the hook with the whole Gunpowder rebellion!

The murdered king is discovered

The king/God link is further developed when Macduff reenters the scene and tells Macbeth and Lennox what he has just witnessed:

> *Most sacrilegious murder hath broke ope*
> *The Lord's annointed temple...*

Sacrilege is the violation or misuse of sacred, holy things: in this case, the murder of the sacred king. Duncan's body is described as the 'Lord's annointed temple' because the king has been annointed as God's representative.

Duncan is more than just a person who has been crowned: his body is sacred, like a holy temple. His murder would have been seen in the same way as going into a church and smashing up the altar. A direct violation of the Christian faith.

Macbeth exits to see for himself and there is much further mayhem. On her entrance, Lady Macbeth's response is rather underwhelming: 'Woe, alas! / What, in our house?' Banquo quickly responds. 'Too cruel, anywhere.' Good point, Banquo - he might see this as odd that Lady Macbeth seems more concerned at where it has happened, than what has happened.

What we need to remember is that only moments before, Macbeth and his wife were standing in the very same spot covered in Duncan's blood. We can forgive them not acting as they might otherwise.

Macbeth, on the other hand, plays his part to perfection. His melodramatic but utterly meaningless words are in keeping with the horror that all have just witnessed:

> All is but toys: renown and grace is dead
> The wine of life is drawn, and the mere lees
> Is left this vault to brag of.

The lees are the dregs left over when the wine barrel has been emptied - Macbeth is saying that there is nothing left of life now that the king is dead.

Notice though that the other characters don't speak in such poetic, grand terms: when Donalbain asks 'What is amiss?', Macbeth replies, 'The spring, the head, the fountain of your blood / Is stopp'd; the very source of it is stopp'd.' Macduff is a little more matter of fact: 'Your royal father's murder'd.'

Is Macbeth overdoing it here with the drama? Trying to make it seem obvious that he is horrified? Possibly: and it is also possible that Banquo suspects something, as he will know Macbeth well and knows him as a down to earth warrior and not a poet.

Cleaning up the evidence

Macbeth then admits that he has just killed the two servants in a fit of blind rage at what they have done. Again, his reasoning is somewhat over-the-top, and you can imagine the other men looking at one another and thinking 'what is he on about?'

He speaks of how Duncan was lying there with his 'silver skin laced with his golden blood' and the servants, 'steep'd in the colours of their trade, their daggers / Unmannerly breached with gore'. In other words, Duncan was lying there stabbed and the two servants were covered in his blood with the daggers in their hands.

Lady Macbeth, perhaps sensing that Macbeth is rather over acting, cries for help, probably feinting, to distract the men away from her husband. You can almost imagine her looking at Macbeth when he speaks and trying to get him to stop talking. Less is more, Macbeth. Don't overdo it.

The last words of Banquo in this scene are important. He says to the men, 'let us meet, / And question this most bloody piece of work, / To know it further.' He is not content with the simple explanation that the two servants were responsible: he believes that 'treasonous malice' is in evidence, and he wants to find out more.

Malcolm and Donalbain decide to flee the country, fearing for their lives. 'There's daggers in men's smiles', Donalbain says. Malcolm doesn't believe that this is over - 'This murderous shaft that's shot / Hath not yet lighted.' An arrow has been fired but has not yet landed.

Of course, at this stage no one directly suspects Macbeth: but everyone is hyper aware that this may not yet be over…

And of course they'd be right! The Macbeths are only just getting started.

ACT 2, SCENE 4

Nature in rebellion

Remember what we just talked about? How nature itself is in torment because of the king's murder? We get a further reminder of it at the start of this scene.

This is what we get at the start of Act 2 Scene 4. Ross and an old man are talking outside the castle gate. Who is this random old man and what purpose does he have? Honestly, it's only to reinforce this point about nature. The old man says that 'this sore night / Hath tempered former knowings': the murder has messed with how they expect the world to work.

> *'Tis unnatural,*

> *Even like the deed that's done. On Tuesday last,*
> *A falcon, towering in her pride of place*
> *Was by a mousing owl hawk'd at and kill'd.*

A large and normally terrifying bird of prey, one at the top of the food chain, was killed by a much smaller bird. He goes on to say that Duncan's horses, normally 'beauteous and swift… turn'd wild in nature, broke their stalls…'

The natural world has been turned upside down by this regicide. Of course it has - you don't murder someone linked directly to God and expect things to go on as normal.

I personally think Shakespeare gets somewhat carried away when the old man says of the horses 'Tis said they eat each other,' to which Ross replies 'They did so.' Really? The horses ate each other? We can forgive Shakespeare some poetic license here as he is trying to reinforce the message to the audience that killing kings isn't a very good idea. I think he succeeds.

Macduff enters, and we have what we call expository dialogue - explanatory dialogue that is there just to fill in the blanks before Act 3. Malcolm and Donalbain have fled, therefore 'the suspicion falls on them' for the murder, and Macbeth will be made king.

ACT 3

ACT 3, SCENE 1

Banquo suspects....

We won't be surprised to know that Banquo is the first person to suspect something fishy about Duncan's murder. He begins by saying 'Thou hast it now…and, I fear / Thou play'dst most foully for't.'

It's not all about Macbeth though: Banquo has his own ambitions. In the same way that the witches prophesied that Macbeth would be king, they said that Banquo himself 'should be the root and father / Of many kings.' The fact that the witches were correct about Macbeth, so he hopes the same happens to him.

Banquo the 'chief guest'

Why is it that both Macbeth and Lady Macbeth suddenly make such a big song and dance about Banquo's presence at that evening's feast? Macbeth calls him 'our chief guest' and Lady Macbeth adds, 'If he had been forgotten / It had been a gap in our feast / An all-thing unbecoming.'

What we can deduce from this is that the Macbeths see Banquo as a threat, and need to get rid of him. They want to put him at ease by flattering him, followed by a seemingly casual enquiry as to whether he goes out riding that afternoon (and how far).

From line 33 Macbeth mentions the news that Malcolm and Donalbain 'are bestow'd in England and Ireland, not confessing / Their cruel parricide' (parricide is the murder of a father by their child). Of course, this is all just a pretence to the next question, as to whether Fleance, Banquo's son, also rides with him.

Macbeth is not interested in Banquo joining the feast, nor about discussing Duncan's sons. He only wants to know where Banquo and his son will be that afternoon, and for how long.

And how do we know this? Because at the moment Macbeth is alone, he begins his next major soliloquy.

To be safely thus....

Macbeth has what he wants: he is king of Scotland. But as far as he is concerned this is meaningless whilst Banquo and Fleance are alive. 'To be thus is nothing,' he says - he has to be 'safely thus'.

Why? Because of the witches' prophecy, one that Banquo has conveniently just reminded us of at the start of the scene (if you were wondering why that was there, now you know). Remember: Banquo's descendants will be kings. Maybe Fleance, maybe one of Fleance's future sons. That doesn't matter - all Macbeth can think of is this:

> *Upon my head they placed a fruitless crown,*
> *And put a barren sceptre in my gripe,*
> *Thence to be wrench'd with an unlineal hand,*
> *No son of mine succeeding.*

Macbeth has no children, so being king is meaningless to him if all he is doing is waiting for Banquo to remove him and put his own children in Macbeth's place.

Any semblance of humanity seems already to have left Macbeth: unlike his deliberations over Duncan's murder, there is no thought to Banquo's honour, kindness or friendship. This is a cold act of premeditated murder, nothing more.

Planning Banquo's murder

The two murderers who enter are not your usual mercenary killers, hired to do a job and no questions asked. It would appear that these are men who fought with Macbeth and Banquo and who were denied a promotion they believed rightfully theirs.

They'd originally believed that this denial was Macbeth's decision, but Macbeth has persuaded them that it was in fact Banquo who had stopped their promotion. 'Know / That it was he in the times past which held you so under fortune' - know that it was in fact Banquo who kept your fortunes down.

Macbeth then challenges the men: 'Do you find / Your patience so predominant in your nature / That you can let this go?' Their reply - 'We are men, my liege' - is a simple response: of course we cannot let this go, as no man could.

This is further challenged by Macbeth, who is clearly trying to wind them up to committing this act by using a similar technique that Lady Macbeth used on him before Duncan's murder. He challenges their idea of manhood.

> *Ay, in the catalogue ye go for men;*
> *As hounds and greyhounds, mongrels, spaniels, curs…*
> *…are clept all by the name of dogs.*

You say you're men, but there are different types of men just as there are different types of dog. So which kind of man are you? It's a direct challenge to their manhood, and, as before, it works a treat.

From line 109 Macbeth is basically saying 'if you are the right type of men, I can give you the business of murdering your enemy, which will bring you closer to our love.'

So, a double benefit - getting rid of the man who Macbeth says denied them, and bringing them closer to Macbeth. Both lies, of course, but we have seen a shift in Macbeth since he became king: he thinks of nothing of saying and doing whatever it takes to keep his crown.

The murderers' response is a little stereotypical: it would appear that Shakespeare didn't take too much time to think about their motivation. They both say that they are sick of life, and don't care what they do to 'spite the world'.

They are probably both battle-worn, hardened by the horrors they've most likely seen in war, and now forgotten by society. The perfect candidates to perform Macbeth's dirty work.

Macbeth's reason for not killing Banquo himself is interesting. 'I could / With barefaced power sweep him from my sight,' he begins. 'Yet I must not', because there are 'certain friends whose loves I may not drop'.

He can't risk losing some of the people close to him by showing himself a murderer in their sight. Of course this is rubbish: he can't murder Banquo because *Banquo has done nothing wrong*. He is a good, honourable man, respected by all, and Macbeth has no reason to get rid of him other than what the witches told them both.

After the Murderers agree, Macbeth explains what needs to happen. He will tell them within the next hour where they need to position themselves, reminds them that they need to leave no trace, and that Fleance must also be killed.

Notice how much colder and harder Macbeth is now. When he finally decided to kill Duncan his mind was in torture. Now, he simply ends 'It is decided.' The humanity he previously had has now deserted him. He is prepared to kill a good friend to remain in power, even though Banquo has shown no signs of rebellion.

Further down the slippery slope he goes…

ACT 3, SCENE 2

Macbeth stands alone

It's interesting to see how Macbeth changes once he has the crown. This is most apparent in the relationship with his wife. Prior to Duncan's murder, we see a man full of doubt who needs Lady Macbeth to give him the courage and motivation he needs to go through with it.

What a difference a crown makes! Let's have a look at this important duologue to see what has shifted in the power dynamic between them.

Before Macbeth's arrival, Lady Macbeth gives us an insight into her troubled mind:

> *Nought's had, all's spent,*
> *Where our desire is got without content:*
> *'Tis safer to be that which we destroy*
> *Than by destruction dwell in doubtful joy.*

They have what they desired, and now rule Scotland. But they are not contented, so what was the point of it? To Lady Macbeth it is better to be Duncan, at peace in his grave, than to be king and queen but to be filled with doubt.

Whereas it was Macbeth who was filled with doubts before, now it would appear the roles have reversed, and it is his wife who wonders what the point of it was.

When Macbeth enters we get the first indication that things are not too good between the two of them. Lady Macbeth asks 'why do you keep alone': it is clear that Macbeth has distanced himself from her. No wonder she is unhappy: she's probably quite lonely.

She ends by saying 'what's done is done': she obviously thinks he is distancing himself and looking stressed because the thoughts of Duncan's murder still haunt him. Far from it - that just shows how little she understands him now. She knows nothing about the meeting with the murderers or the plan to kill Banquo and Fleance.

For a woman as controlling as Lady Macbeth, that must be torture! We will see the effect this has on her later.

Macbeth's growing paranoia

Macbeth explains why he is still so uneasy. 'We have scotch'd the snake, not killed it,' he says: the snake being any opposition or challenge to his throne. What follows is classic paranoid speak: this snake has been injured, but lies in wait to bite them.

They will 'eat our meal in fear and sleep / In the affliction of these terrible dreams': their lives lived in fear of someone attempting on them what they did to Duncan. Macbeth then echoes Lady Macbeth's words above:

> ...better be with the dead,
> Whom we, to gain our peace, have sent to peace,
> Than on the torture of the mind to lie
> In restless ecstacy.

It's better to be dead and at peace than to live in this torture. Now that you know some of the historical context of the play, it's interesting to see just how much Shakespeare is warning anyone from committing regicide! Talk about signing a one way ticket to unhappiness and paranoia....

It's also important that we see Macbeth's unhappiness, as it ensures we still have some sympathy for him. If he suddenly turned into an unfeeling psychopath who gained pleasure from this suffering and enjoyed killing people, we'd feel pretty distant from him. But even though he's no longer in anguish because of the murder of Duncan, he's still filled with pain.

Lady Macbeth, sensing she is losing control of her husband, does the only thing she can - tells him to calm down and prepare for the meal, as she needs him to be an excellent host. His response - telling her to do the same thing - shows that he no longer needs her counsel.

What Macbeth says next is quite strange. He tells Lady Macbeth to pay extra attention to Banquo at the meal that night. But surely Banquo is about to be murdered, so why bother to say this to her?

Two possible reasons: either he wishes to totally keep the murder plan from her, or he is worried it will backfire. The first of these is more likely - perhaps he wants to offer her 'plausible deniability' - the less she knows the better? Or the less she knows, the less control she has over the situation. I think this is most likely.

Be innocent of the knowledge…

However, Macbeth does hint that, before nightfall 'there shall be done / A deed of dreadful note.' When Lady Macbeth asks what this is, Macbeth's response is telling: 'Be innocent of the knowledge, dearest chuck, / Till thou applaud the deed.'

Now, call me an enlightened 21st Century male, but doesn't that sound ever-so-slightly patronising to you? It's pretty much him saying 'don't you worry about it, dear, and thank me when you find out what it is'. Lady Macbeth seems to have fulfilled her purpose - he no longer needs her. She has lost her power within the marriage, and what is even more interesting, has lost her voice.

She says nothing more in this scene, and, other than trying to keep order during the banquet when Macbeth sees Banquo's ghost, will have little else to say until she is seen sleepwalking towards the play's end.

We'll look into her character in a little more detail in a later section.

ACT 3, SCENE 3

Banquo's murder

This starts in an interesting way. A Third Murderer joins the two that Macbeth has tasked with killing Banquo and his son. The First Murderer asks who sent him: he replies 'Macbeth'. This annoys the

Second Murderer, who comments 'He needs not our mistrust': Macbeth should trust us.

Some commentators have suggested that this Third Murderer might be Macbeth in disguise, who has joined the other two to ensure they get the job done. It's impossible to say for sure, but based on what we know about Macbeth it makes sense. The fact that the Third Murderer so confidently says 'Tis he' when he sees Banquo also suggests he knows the victim.

The scene is over with quickly: Banquo is 'set upon' and murdered, and Fleance escapes. With the torch put out it is impossible for them to know where Fleance has gone.

ACT 3, SCENE 4

The banquet

The scene begins with Macbeth and Lady Macbeth playing the role of generous hosts. The warm and friendly atmosphere is punctuated by the murderers showing up and Macbeth telling one of them he has blood on his face. He asks whether the men killed Banquo, which they confirm. However, when they tell him Fleance escaped he is naturally concerned.

> *Then comes my fit again: I had all else been perfect…*
> *But now I am cabin'd, cribb'd, confined, bound in*
> *To saucy doubts and fears.*

He feels that while Fleance lives he is imprisoned by doubt: he cannot be free until the boy is dead. Notice the alliteration adding to this sense of confinement: the words sound hard and cold. However, 'the worm that's fled' is still too young to cause him problems - he has 'no teeth for the present'. Macbeth will deal with him later.

Lady Macbeth calls her husband back into the banquet - he has an important role to play and being distracted does not allow him to do so. This is an important event for the Macbeths and he cannot be seen to mess it up.

The ghost appears

What follows is one of the most famous scenes in all Shakespeare. Banquo's ghost appears and sits in Macbeth's place. Ross invites Macbeth to sit. Macbeth asks where: as far as he is concerned there are no free places. When he sees Banquo, he asks 'Which of you have done this?... never shake / Thy gory locks at me.'

As far as everyone else in the banqueting hall knows, Macbeth is talking to an empty chair. Ross asks everyone to rise, but Lady Macbeth tells them to sit, saying 'my lord is often thus, /And hath been from his youth.'

She tries to make an excuse - nothing to worry about, just something that happens from time to time. She calls it a 'fit' and says it's 'momentary'. If they pay him too much attention it will 'extend his passion' - make it worse. Not easy trying to continue your meal while the king is shouting at an empty chair.

She turns to Macbeth and utters her usual motivator: 'Are you a man?...This is the very painting of your fear: / This is the air-drawn dagger..' She doesn't know what Macbeth has seen, knows nothing of Banquo's murder - as far as she is concerned, Macbeth is still having hallucinations due to stress.

But we know otherwise: perhaps it is Macbeth's guilt, or perhaps the ghost really is there (it's not the first time Shakespeare has used a ghost - Hamlet's father visits him at the start of the play). Either way, Macbeth is seeing the results of his actions in the last place he wants to see them - in front of everyone he has to convince of the stability of his rule.

Lady Macbeth continues (of course): she compares Macbeth's apparent fear to 'A woman's story at a winter's fire' - he is behaving like a woman telling a story by a fire.

Of course, Macbeth is not convinced, as Banquo continues to sit there and look up at him. He says to her 'see there! behold! look! lo!' He is amazed that she cannot see anything.

Her response continues in the same way - 'What, quite unmann'd in folly?' - has your foolishness made you lose your manhood? Surely by now she must realise that this strategy no longer words. Macbeth is well beyond reacting to this approach.

It is when she reminds Macbeth that he has guests who are all looking at him in horror that he snaps out of it. 'I do forget,' he says. 'Do not muse at me.... I have a strange infirmity, which is nothing / To those that know me.' Banquo then leaves Macbeth's seat and disappears for a few moments. This allows Macbeth to sit down and have some wine.

Banquo reappears

However, it isn't long before Banquo reappears, and Macbeth once again shouts in fear at this apparition. 'Thy bones are marrowless, they blood is cold' he says to the ghost. How is it possible for a dead man to reappear like this? As we've said, this is either a ghost genuinely appearing, or we are witnessing Macbeth's mental deterioration.

By the time the ghost once more disappears, the party atmosphere is ruined. 'You have displaced the mirth, broke the good meeting, /With most admired disorder' Lady Macbeth says. What Macbeth cannot understand is how she managed to stay so calm throughout - he believes she could also see the ghost but that she was able to keep 'the natural ruby of your cheeks'.

When Ross begins to question what Macbeth saw, Lady Macbeth decides to end the banquet before her husband says too much.

Blood will have blood...

Macbeth and Lady Macbeth are alone on stage. Macbeth begins by saying 'It will have blood; they say, blood will have blood'. We've seen the image of blood a lot thus far in the play: it is linked to many different thematic elements. In this case, blood refers to death - these acts Macbeth has committed will lead to his own death.

Macbeth has to know his fate; and this means a visit to the 'weird sisters'. He also needs to know what Macduff's actions are - as he keeps a spy in Macduff's house he can easily find out.

This is a real turning point in the play: Macbeth tells his wife that he has gone too far now to turn back:

> *I am in blood*
> *Stepp'd in so far that, should I wade no more,*
> *Returning were as tedious as go o'er.*

He has waded through so much blood that it is pointless him turning back now. He's in it for the duration, whatever he has to do to stay in power.

All Lady Macbeth is able to say in response is that he needs sleep. Macbeth agrees, but ends the scene with the chilling 'We are yet but young in deed'.

There is a lot more to come...

ACT 3, SCENE 5

The Witches meet Hecate

In this short scene, Hecate, the goddess of witchcraft, meets the three witches. You may actually find that this scene isn't in your version of the play and for good reason: many modern commentators don't think it was written by Shakespeare but was inserted at a later date.

There are a few reasons why people now doubt this scene. Firstly, it's written in tetrameter (four beats per line) not Shakespeare's standard pentameter (five beats). Secondly, the witches don't come across in the same sinister way as in Act 1. Thirdly, what they sing was actually written by Thomas Middleton, another playwright of the time - it features in his play, 'The Witches'. So Middleton himself may have written the scene.

So, make your own mind up on it, but I'm pretty sure this scene was not written by the Bard. And the play is better off without it in my opinion.

ACT 3, SCENE 6

Remember the closing scene of Act 2, where we had the old man speaking to Ross and explaining how nature seemed to be rebelling because of Duncan's murder? Well, we have a similar technique being used here, in the closing scene of Act 3.

By now, word is out that Macbeth has played foul to get the kingship. The Scottish Lords are beginning to wonder out loud why so many people around Macbeth have recently ended up dead.

Lennox gives voice to these concerns. In his speech, which is heavily ironic, almost sarcastic in its tone, he questions why it is that Duncan was pitied by Macbeth after his death, why Banquo ended up dead just because he stayed out late, why Fleance is now accused of Banquo's murder just because he ran away, why Malcolm and Donalbain are also accused because they did the same thing, and why Macbeth killed the servants in a 'pious rage'.

Macbeth's lies and his inability to maintain a 'game face' has led the Scottish lords to believe that he has had a hand in all of this. These suspicions have been most likely brought on by the lords seeing Macbeth shouting at a stool and then discovering later that evening that Banquo has been murdered.

Notice though that Lennox doesn't come straight out and say all this: he probably feels he cannot, as Scotland is a dangerous place under Macbeth's rule. Instead, he heavily implies that it is just too much of a coincidence that all this has happened under Macbeth's watch. A case of being able to put two and two together.

The Lord then explains that Macduff has gone to England, where Malcolm is under the protection of 'the most pious Edward' (the English king). Macduff has gone there to raise an army to attack

Macbeth, so that 'we may again / Give to our tables meat, sleep to our nights, / Free from our feasts and banquets bloody knives'.

This suggests that not only do the Scottish people live in fear of these 'bloody knives', but there is also famine, showing once again how nature has turned on the people through the unnatural act of killing king Duncan.

Macbeth had better watch his back - the knives are out and are being sharpened...

ACT 4

ACT 4, SCENE 1

The Witches' spell

Much of this is pretty familiar, as it's what we typically think of when we think about witches in general. The cauldron, the strange ingredients, the chanting. The Witches speak in **trochaic tetrameter** - lines of four beats, with the stress on the **first** syllable of each foot rather than the **second** (known as a **trochee**). The capitals denote where the stress falls on each syllable:

DEE dum DEE dum DEE dum DEE.

This is opposed to the iambic meter most of Shakespeare's writing is in, where the stress falls on the second syllable:

Dum DEE dum DEE dum DEE dum ... and so on

Can you hear this when you read the chanting out loud?

ROUND aBOUT the CAULdron GO

IN the POISon'd ENtrails THROW

I hope so. Why does Shakespeare change his normal meter for the spell? Because it has an incessant, driving rhythm that adds power to the words. It isn't the sort of musical poetry we hear in much of the rest of the play: it's almost childlike, like a nursery rhyme:

JACK and JILL went UP the HILL.

See what I mean?

Look at the ingredients that go into the pot: poison'd entrails, toad's venom, newt's eyes, dog's tongue and so on. We can sense that the spell they are brewing up will be an evil one. And of course we'd be right - Macbeth is about to appear and they know what he will ask them. They'd better make this spell count.

Something wicked this way comes...

The Second Witch announces Macbeth's arrival by saying 'something wicked this way comes'. Macbeth must have sunk pretty low by now for these evil creatures to recognise how wicked he now is.

Macbeth gets straight to the point: he doesn't care how much destruction it causes, whether the Witches 'untie the winds', or 'the yesty waves / Confound and swallow navigation up', or even 'castles topple on their warders' heads'. He has to know what is in store for him.

The First Witch asks Macbeth whether he wants to hear it from them, or their 'masters': by this she means those evil spirits that Lady Macbeth herself conjured up at the start of the play. Remember: during the time that the play was written people believed that there were evil spirits in the world, and even that women became witches by having sex with the devil.

Macbeth would have wanted to hear his future direct from the horse's mouth, as it were. This would have been pretty terrifying for an audience to hear at that time.

The three Apparitions

Three Apparitions then appear to tell Macbeth his future. The first (an armed head) tells him to beware Macduff. The second (a bloody child) explains that 'none of woman born / Shall harm Macbeth'. The third (a child crowned with a tree in his hand) explains that Macbeth will not be beaten until 'Great Birnam Wood to High Dunsinane Hill / Shall come against him.'

What does all this mean? Essentially, what this means is that Macbeth thinks he is invincible. Everyone is born, he reasons, so Macduff can't be that much of a threat. And an entire forest approaching his castle? Impossible!

However, there is hidden meaning in the three Apparitions. The armed (helmeted head) represents Macbeth's head, that will be cut off by Macduff at the end of the play.

The bloody child represents Macduff, who has indeed been ripped from his mother's womb so not born in the conventional sense, and the child crowned is Fleance. Whilst their words seem to offer Macbeth some comfort, there is irony in the images that present these visions of the future.

But Macbeth is not yet satisfied - he has to know - 'shall Banquo's issue ever reign in this kingdom?' He is still obsessed by Fleance. But the Witches have told him all they can for now - 'Seek to know no more' they say. Macbeth is unhappy about this - 'Let me know!' he says.

Instead, they show him *'Eight Kings, the last with a glass in his hand, Ghost of Banquo following'*. These eight kings are the heirs of Banquo, which further shows Macbeth his failure. 'The blood-bolter'd Banquo smiles upon me, / And points at them for his' - Banquo points to the kings as if telling Macbeth they are his descendants.

After a short dance the Witches vanish. At this moment Lennox enters. Macbeth asks whether Lennox had seen the Witches. Lennox tells him no, but that Macduff has fled for England. Macbeth curses his lack of speed in deciding to kill Macduff: 'from this moment, /

The very firstlings of my heart shall be / The firstlings of my hand' - I'll act as soon as I think.

Macbeth will have Macduff's wife and children killed - anyone who could lay claim to the throne in future. He has become obsessed with eradicating anyone who might in future take away his crown.

Lower and lower he sinks. When will this end?

ACT 4, SCENE 2

The murder of Lady Macduff and family

In true dramatic fashion, we then cut straight to the scene where Lady Macduff and kids are murdered. You can sense things speeding up now: as in any good thriller movie, the final act is getting close and the walls are closing in.

Lady Macduff asks her cousin Ross why her husband has fled Scotland. Ross has no answer - but as far as Lady Macduff is concerned this is pure madness: it 'runs against all reason' to leave them there. She is clearly terrified of what Macbeth will do.

And well she might be. After Ross leaves, Lady Macduff has a conversation with her son about the fact that, as far as she is concerned, Macduff is dead. A pretty harsh thing to say to a son, but she is so terrified for all their lives that she has resigned herself to the fact that she'll never see Macduff again.

Her son is rather mature in his response: 'how will you do for a husband?' he says, to which she replies 'Why, I can buy me twenty at any market'. She is so upset with Macduff that she is pretty sure she can get herself a replacement quite easily - she clearly doesn't rate men much at this point, and who'd blame her. It does seem that she's been deserted at the worst possible time.

Somewhat bizarrely, a Messenger then shows up and tells Lady Macduff that she is in danger and 'hence, with your little ones' - get away with your children. Lady Macduff's response is rather pathetic - 'Whither should I fly? / I have done no harm.' She has nowhere to go and no idea what she has done to deserve being in such danger.

The Murderers then appear: we don't know if it's the same men as before, and frankly it doesn't matter. Macbeth is now paying people to do his dirty work for him.

Modern versions of the play tend to omit the end of this scene, as we aren't that keen on seeing the murder of children, for very obvious reasons.

However, in Shakespeare's day audiences were less worried about these sorts of gory details, so this would have happened on stage. Lady Macduff's son is stabbed, his last words to tell his mother to 'Run away'. As you can imagine, there's no chance of that.

ACT 4, SCENE 3

Macduff and Malcolm speak of the state of Scotland

The first 160 lines of this long scene are a little tedious to be honest. Malcolm and Macduff discuss the state of Scotland under Macbeth: 'Bleed, bleed, poor country!' Macduff says, echoing the blood motif we've seen throughout. Scotland is dying, and Macbeth must be stopped.

Strangely, Malcolm then says that, compared to how he'd be if he was king, Macbeth is a pussycat:

> *When I shall tread upon the tyrant's head,*
> *Or wear it on my sword, yet my poor country*
> *Shall have more vices than it had before,*
> *More suffer and more sundry ways than ever,*
> *By him that shall succeed.*

When he stands on Macbeth's head or has it on his sword, Scotland will be even more filled with vice and will suffer even more. When Malcolm becomes king:

> *Your wives, your daughters,*
> *Your matrons and your maids, could not fill up*
> *The cistern of my lust…*

What on earth is he saying to Macduff? That when he is king he will be even worse than Macbeth? Macduff tries to soften Malcolm's words, saying that 'there cannot be / That vulture in you, to devour so many…'

But Malcolm keeps going on about how awful he is, saying that he would 'cut off the nobles for their lands, / Desire his jewels and this other's house…', And that all this 'would make me hunger more'.

Macduff (bless him) still tries to comfort Malcolm, telling him that there is plenty in Scotland to 'fill up your will', and that Malcolm's other qualities will outweigh these negative points.

But no! As far as Malcolm is concerned he has none of the qualities a king should have. Macduff gives up, crying 'O Scotland, Scotland!' He's clearly feeling pretty worried about the state of the country if someone as awful as Malcolm succeeds Macbeth.

Macduff then speaks to his country, giving an impassioned plea for a decent ruler who can give Scotland hope again:

> *O nation miserable…*
> *When shalt thou see thy wholesome days again,*
> *Since that the truest issue of thy throne*
> *By his own interdiction stands accursed,*
> *And does blaspheme his breed?*

Poor Scotland, when will you see good days again, when the one person who has most right to the throne has, in his own words, cursed himself, and destroyed his own royalty with his words?

He has a point. Out of the frying pan into the fire, it would seem.

But never fear! Because it was all a cunning plan by Malcolm to bring out Macduff's most loyal and patriotic tendencies (you have to wonder why Malcolm bothered, which is why this scene is often drastically cut in performances of the play).

> ...this noble passion... hath from my soul
> Wiped the black scruples, reconciled my thoughts
> To thy good truth and honour.

Your fundamental goodness has removed all these terrible, dark thoughts from me.

He goes on to say that he has never actually been with a woman, has never really been greedy, and has never broken his faith. So what was the point of lying like that above? Macduff isn't sure himself: 'Such welcome and unwelcome things at once / 'Tis hard to reconcile.' It's no surprise he's confused - we are as well.

Malcolm simply says 'Well, more anon,' which I guess leaves Macduff still scratching his head. Don't worry if you're doing the same - it's a bizarre and slightly random scene.

The scene moves into its second phase when Ross arrives and tells Macduff that his wife and children have been murdered. Again, it's a really strange scene, as initially Macduff asks Ross how his wife and children are. Ross replies 'Well'. When Macduff asks for more detail, Ross says that they were 'well at peace when I did leave 'em.'

What does he mean here? 'At peace' is another way of saying dead. Is Ross alluding to the fact that Lady Macduff and son are indeed dead?

After Ross tells Macduff that he is needed back in Scotland ('your eye in Scotland / Would create soldiers, make our women fight'), Macduff replies that 'We are coming thither'. England has lent them 'good Siward and ten thousand men'. They are on their way back to fight Macbeth.

Ross then breaks the news:

> *I have words*
> *That would be howl'd out in the desert air,*

> *Where hearing should not latch them…*
> *Your castle is surprised; your wife and babes*
> *Savagely slaughtered…*

Macduff cannot believe what he is hearing: 'My wife kill'd too?… All my pretty ones? Did you say all?'

Malcolm urges him to 'make us medicines of our great revenge, / To cure this deadly grief': he wants Macduff to take the pain he feels and turn it into revenge, in order to cure the grief he feels. He wants Macduff to 'Dispute it like a man'. As far as Malcolm is concerned, the correct emotion to display here is the violent wish for revenge.

However, Macduff tells him that he 'must also feel it as a man'. There is nothing wrong with men feeling grief and pain, and showing it. This is a very different side to masculinity and endears us to Macduff.

Again Malcolm encourages Macduff to 'let grief convert to anger; blunt not the heart, enrage it.' It's clear that Malcolm can see an opportunity here, to take these raw emotions and turn them into something of use to him in his attack on Macbeth.

And it seems to work: 'Bring thou this fiend of Scotland and myself; / Within my sword's length set him'. Just get me in the room with the man and he'll feel the point of my sword.

'This tune goes manly,' Malcolm replies. A manly thing to say.

ACT 5

ACT 5, SCENE 1

Out out damned spot…

This is the famous sleepwalking scene, where a Doctor and Gentlewoman (one of Lady Macbeth's serving women) observe the Queen confessing her and her husband's sins.

The Doctor begins by questioning when the Gentlewoman last saw the Queen sleepwalk: he has been watching with her for two nights and has seen nothing yet. The Gentlewoman tells him that she has seen the Queen get out of bed, unlock her closet, take out a pen, begin writing, read it, seal it and then go back to bed.

This is a very complex thing for a sleepwalking woman to do! The Doctor notes this, calling it a 'great perturbation in nature': another example of how Shakespeare shows the Macbeths' acts to be against nature itself.

The Doctor asks the woman what she has heard the Queen say during these nocturnal sessions. The woman refuses to tell him, saying that there is 'no witness' to confirm what she has heard.

Suddenly, the Queen appears. The Doctor asks what she is doing rubbing her hands: the gentlewoman explains that 'It is an accustomed action with her, to seem thus washing her hands: I have known her continue in this a quarter of an hour'.

Why is she pretending to wash her hands? Of course, she believes there is something on her hands that she cannot remove. 'Yet here's a spot,' she says, looking at her hands. 'Out damned spot! Out, I say!' She cannot remove the blood from her hands - the guilt at the murders and the lies that have got them to where they are now.

The words that follow indicate to the Doctor exactly the role they played in the murders of Duncan and Lady Macduff:

Yet who would have thought the old man to have had so much blood in him... The thane of Fife had a wife: where is she now?

Notice that Lady Macbeth does not speak in the iambic pentameter blank verse that we have become used to seeing the important characters speak: this shows us the unstructured nature of her nocturnal confessions. She is no longer speaking in poetry - this is the unfiltered contents of her tormented mind.

She repeats how she cannot get the stains from her hands:

What, will these hands ne'er be clean?...all the perfumes of Arabia will not sweeten this little hand.

There is no way she can remove the past - she is stained by it. Her unconscious mind in sleep gives away the anguish she feels. She names Banquo as one who 'cannot come out on's grave' and then heads back to bed, remembering the knocking at the gate after Duncan's murder.

When Lady Macbeth leaves, the Doctor once more reminds us of the unnaturalness of what he has just witnessed: 'unnatural deeds / Do breed unnatural troubles'.

The strength that Lady Macbeth demonstrated at the start of the play has finally left her: she is a broken, lonely woman who is losing her mind. Far worse than any heroic death, defending her honour, she will die a desperately lonely and tragic figure, isolated from her husband and with nothing left to live for.

As we have seen before, Shakespeare continually reminds us of the awful consequences for anyone who might dare to kill a king. It is in many ways a deeply instructive play. No wonder King James liked it so much.

ACT 5, SCENE 2

In this short scene, Mentieth, Angus, Caithness and Lennox plan the attack against Macbeth. Mentieth mentions that the English army are getting closer and that 'revenges burn in them'. They will meet the army near Birnam Wood.

Shakespeare manages to maintain a little sympathy for Macbeth:

> *Now does he feel*
> *His secret murders sticking on his hands…. Now does he feel*
>   *his title*
> *Hang loose about him, like a giant's robe*
> *Upon a dwarfish thief.*

Macbeth feels the past lying heavily on him. This is not a man in complete delusion, but rather one who is desperately trying to hold on to what is not rightfully his.

They march on to Birnam, to meet the English army, Macduff and Malcolm…

ACT 5, SCENE 3

Macbeth has been off stage for some time, and the man we now see has once more changed. He seems obsessed with the witches' prophecy:

> *Bring me no more reports; let them fly all:*
> *Till Birnam wood remove to Dunsinane,*

> *I cannot taint with fear. What's the boy Malcolm?*
> *Was he not born of woman?*

As far as he is concerned, he doesn't need to worry until Birnam wood comes to his castle and he confronts someone who wasn't born. And what are the chances of that? Macbeth is filled with a false confidence that will ultimately prove fatal.

He is rude to servant boy who tries to tell him that English soldiers are approaching the castle. We then get an insight into the depths of his unhappiness: he says he is 'sick at heart' and that the army's approach will either give him peace or remove him from his throne.

We sense him feeling sorry for himself when he says:

> *…that which should accompany old age,*
> *As honour, love, obedience, troops of friends,*
> *I must not look to have.*

Like his wife, Macbeth is lonely, with no love in his life and with no one showing him the honour he believes he deserves. He has resigned himself this, made his pact with the devil and has to take the consequences.

Much of Shakespeare's genius comes in us feeling some connection with Macbeth even now, after he has committed such terrible acts. The fact that Macbeth is able to reflect on his life in such a poetic and thoughtful way means we cannot feel total dislike for him. This continues until the end.

However, the old warrior Macbeth soon returns when he says 'I'll fight till from my bones my flesh be hacked.' This is not a man who will hide behind his army - he is prepared to go into battle to defend his title.

The Doctor arrives, and tells Macbeth that his wife is 'troubled with thick coming fancies'. Macbeth's reply is blunt: 'Cure her of that' - he expects the Doctor to be able to 'Pluck from the memory a rooted sorrow'. However, the Doctor rightly tells him that 'Therein the patient / Must minister to himself'. There are some things a doctor cannot cure.

Macbeth calls for his armour to be put on, and tells the Doctor that if he can 'find her disease' and get rid of it he will be hugely thanked. Clearly Macbeth is greatly worried about his wife even in the midst of these preparations for battle, once again showing that his human side is still there somewhere.

Macbeth ends the scene by repeating his boast that he need not be afraid of death until Birnam wood comes to his castle. He won't have long to wait.

ACT 5, SCENE 4

Another short scene - like in any good movie, the scenes towards the end speed up as we reach the climax. It's as if the camera is cutting between the two scenes of Macbeth in his castle and the approaching army.

And guess what! Malcolm suggests that 'every soldier hew him down a bow' of the trees in Birnam wood in order to 'shadow the numbers of our host'. He wants to hide the size of the army by the front rows carrying tree branches in front of them. Looks like one of the witches' prophecies has come true!

On they march, closer and closer to the castle at Dunsinane.

ACT 5, SCENE 5

In another masterstroke, Shakespeare encourages us to feel sympathy for Macbeth in the moments leading up to his death. This is no mean feat - he's murdered a king, his best friend, and a woman and child. Let's see how Shakespeare manages to pull this off.

We begin with Macbeth's fearless call to arms - he is not afraid of the incoming army, believing that 'our castle's strength / Will laugh a siege to scorn' - his castle is more than a match for this siege.

To-morrow, and to-morrow, and to-morrow

But it is when he is told 'The queen, my lord, is dead', that we see Macbeth for who he truly is now.

Macbeth's final soliloquy is perhaps his most famous, and arguably one of the most powerful speeches ever penned by Shakespeare. It's worth printing in full:

> *To-morrow, and to-morrow, and to-morrow,*
> *Creeps in this petty pace from day to day*
> *To the last syllable of recorded time,*
> *And all our yesterdays are lighted fools*
> *The way to dusty death. Out, out, brief candle!*
> *Life's but a walking shadow, a poor player*
> *That struts and frets his hour upon the stage*
> *And then is heard no more: it is a tale*
> *Told by an idiot, full of sound and fury,*
> *Signifying nothing.*

I don't think anything like that had ever been written before, and there are few writers since who could match this speech for its raw power and beauty.

We get right inside the mind of this tormented tyrant, and what we find is a man who sees no point in anything any more, who sees life as nothing more than a shadow, an actor on stage for his allotted time who then leaves the stage and is 'heard no more', a story told by an idiot, full of noise but ultimately meaningless. That's a pretty bleak assessment.

We'll look more carefully at this and other soliloquies in a later section, where we deconstruct Shakespeare's style.

A messenger appears and tells Macbeth that he has seen Birnam wood move. Macbeth cannot believe it - he tells the messenger he will hang if he is lying. He then combines frantically preparing for battle - 'Arm, arm and out!' with further weary admittance that he is getting pretty fed up of life - 'I gin to be weary of the sun, / And wish the estate o' the world were now undone.'

His final words, however, remind us of Macbeth the warrior - 'Blow wind! Come, wrack! / At least we'll die with harness on our back.'

Let battle commence…

ACT 5 SCENE 6

A super short scene this - Macduff, Malcolm and Siward prepare to attack. They throw down their branches, Siward takes the lead and Malcolm and Macduff follow.

Charge!

ACT 5, SCENE 7

The scene opens with Macbeth reiterating his desire to face them like a man: 'bear-like, I must fight the course.' He once again reminds himself that no one born of a woman can harm him. It's as if he's trying to convince himself that everything will be ok even though one of the prophesies has already been proven.

First up, Young Siward, who is quickly slain by Macbeth. Macbeth exits and Macduff, Siward and Malcolm enter, looking for Macbeth. Shakespeare is clever here: no longer are the characters separated by scenes, but by the simple action of exiting and entering the stage. This shows the audience how much closer they are to one another.

Macduff hears the intense battle with Macbeth and commands 'Tyrant, show thy face!' He has to kill Macbeth himself or 'My wife and children's ghosts will haunt me still.' He will kill Macbeth both for the good of Scotland and also for personal vengeance. This will give the final battle a more dramatic note.

In the same way that Macbeth believes his fate has been written through the witches' prophesies, so Macduff believes that fortune will let him find Macbeth.

And so they enter the castle…

ACT 5, SCENE 8

In the final scene of the play, Macduff confronts Macbeth for one last battle. Macbeth has clearly killed a few enemies, commenting that 'the gashes / Do better upon them.' He refuses to 'play the Roman fool' and die on his sword: he is probably thinking of some Roman Emperor like Cassius or Brutus, who killed themselves when they could see their battle was over.

When Macduff appears and commands Macbeth to 'turn' and face him, Macbeth wearily tells him that he does not want to take his life, as 'my soul is too much charged / With blood of thine already.' He has too much of the Macduff family's blood on his hands to add more.

Macduff's reply -'I have no words: / My voice is in my sword' - reminds us that Macduff is a warrior, not a talker, as Macbeth was before.

The difference is that Macbeth allowed himself to be wooed by words, first by the witches and then by his wife. If he had stuck to being a brave soldier none of this would have happened. Macduff tells him that the time for words is over - only actions now count.

Macbeth then tells Macduff that there is little point in trying to attack him - he is as likely to make a dent 'in the entrenchant air' than make Macbeth bleed, because he bears 'a charmed life', which cannot be ended by 'one of woman born'.

But guess what? Yes, you know! Macduff was 'from his mother's womb / Untimely ripp'd.' He was born by what would have been some sort of rudimentary caesarian section - although we can imagine that his mother did not survive the procedure, or had perhaps died in childbirth.

Macbeth gives an interesting response, which once again refers back to the dominant theme of masculinity:

> *Accursed be the tongue that tells me so,*
> *For it hath cow'd my better part of man!*

Macduff's words have made cowardly that part of Macbeth he needs in order to fight. He has been carried to this point by the witches telling him that he was safe - or at least giving him the impression. But this was all false confidence, and now it has been removed, through all three prophecies being proven, Macbeth has nothing left.

However, there is some fight left in Macbeth, which once more ensures the audience feel some sympathy for Macbeth. He will go down fighting, not yield like a coward. Macbeth will 'try the last'. The exit, fighting.

While they're off, Malcolm, Ross and Siward enter, and Ross tells Siward that his son has been killed. This short dialogue is really only there to give Macduff enough time to chop off Macbeth's head: we don't see this for obvious reasons - not because an Elizabethan audience would have found this disgusting, but more because it's quite hard to stage cutting off someone's head…

Macduff re-enters, holding Macbeth's head and proclaiming Malcolm the next king. Malcolm ends the play by making those thanes who fought with him earls, the first in Scotland. He also promises to bring home any Scots who were 'exiled abroad' during Macbeth's rule - those who fled Scotland for fear of their lives.

He says he will do these things 'and what needed else… in measure, pace and time'. His words seem deliberately calm and measured in contrast with Macbeth's passionate excesses. He not only comes across as a potentially strong king, but as a wily politician: he understands what his people need to hear, and he gives it to them.

Notice also that Malcolm reminds us of the divine right of kings - his direct link to God:

And what needed else

That calls upon us, by the grace of Grace…

That second capitalised Grace is the Grace of God: he has been blessed by God in the way his father had been, but Macbeth had not. Hence the natural world being all over the place during his reign (horses eating each other etc.)

THE END

And that's the end! Well done - we made it. I hope that summary gave you lots of useful detail that you've used to annotate your text. If you haven't done that yet, and preferred to read through this guide first, that's fine - but I would recommend that, as part of your revision, you do mark up your play text in pencil using these notes.

Let's turn our attention now to the characters. There's plenty to say about each.

THE CHARACTERS

WHAT ARE CHARACTERS?

If I was to begin this section by saying that the first thing you need to know about fictional characters is that **they aren't real people**, you'd probably say 'well of course not, even I know that.'

But what you might not have thought about before is what the **purpose** or **function** of different characters is in any fictional narrative.

You see, each character in a novel, play, film or TV show has a purpose. And that purpose is to **move the story onwards**. If a character doesn't do that, he or she has no right to be in that story.

They do this by **creating conflict**, as this is the most important tool a writer has at their disposal. It is only when characters are in conflict with themselves and with those around them that we have a storyline.

By conflict, I don't necessarily mean characters fighting with each other (although we get a fair bit of that in this play). I mean characters who come from different backgrounds, have different opinions, and who want different things. If every character in *Macbeth* agreed with each other it would be rather boring.

No, the reason this play works is because there is so much internal conflict. All of the characters respond differently to the Inspector, and this causes tension.

Let's look at how these characters differ, and how Shakespeare sets up this contrast and conflict in order to explore the main themes of the play.

MACBETH

MACBETH THE TRAGIC HERO

Macbeth is a little more complex than many of Shakespeare's villains. We cannot compare him to the likes of Iago (Othello) and Richard III, men who seem to relish the terrible things they do and who begin the play as misanthropes: people who have a hatred of the world and everyone in it.

Macbeth is harder to pin down, and this is why he has remained one of Shakespeare's most interesting tragic heroes. Let's take a moment to learn a little about what we mean by the term 'tragic hero'. We'll talk more about the tragedy genre in a later section.

The Tragic Hero 'Archetype'

Let's take a moment to talk about the conventions of the tragic hero archetype (the typical tragic hero in literature). Shakespeare certainly didn't invent this character - he's been around since the Greeks.

The word 'hero' comes from the Greek for 'someone who demonstrates courage in the face of adversity or danger'. This is important: you won't have a hero unless they're challenged by something tough or dangerous.

A tragic hero is one who faces this adversity but also encounters their own downfall. This downwards journey should evoke feelings of pity and fear in the audience. This is what gives tragedies their impact: we feel a connection to the hero and travel with them towards their tragic ending.

The emotions the audience feels are what the Greeks called *catharsis*. We still use this word today: we talk about how certain things are cathartic, such as having a good cry when we are feeling overwhelmed/tired/stressed etc. It can help us feel better.

It's also important that the hero has high status, because the higher they are, the further they fall at the end of the play. Romeo, Juliet, Hamlet, Othello, King Lear, Macbeth - all of them hold important positions, or come from important families, at the start of the play.

The tragic hero's downfall may be brought on by bad luck or poor judgement, but it is also a reflection of their fatal flaw, or *hamartia*. This is the aspect of their character that at first may seem positive, but that ultimately results in their death: it is out of this dominant character trait that they make the decisions which causes their downfall.

Think of Romeo's poetic desire for romantic love, causing him to link up with the daughter of his family's sworn enemy. Or Hamlet, whose constant brooding and overthinking causes him to delay plans to revenge his father's death and neglect the women in his life. Or Othello, whose intense, possessive love of his wife Desdemona causes him to believe Iago's lies about her infidelity.

All of Shakespeare's tragic heroes have qualities which turn against them.

Each tragic hero will have a moment of *anagnorisis* late in the play - a moment of discovery. This is when the lights go on and they realise who/what they have become or what is happening to them. The tragedy of this is that it is always too late - their fate has been sealed.

We'll see that with Macbeth, just before he defends his castle from Malcolm and the English army, where he realises that life is just a meaningless act that is over almost before it has begun.

THE SOURCE OF MACBETH'S CHARACTER

As we've mentioned before, the story of Macbeth comes from Holinshed's *Chronicles*, a large, comprehensive description of British history published in 1577 and revised in 1587 (not long before Macbeth was written).

Whilst the key historical points don't change much (other than Holinshed recounting that it was Banquo who helped Macbeth kill king Duncan), what Shakespeare most notably adds is the emotional/psychological journey Macbeth goes on through the play.

This is what differentiates Shakespeare's plays from any that had come before - Shakespeare was the first (and some would still say the greatest) playwright to really delve deep inside the human condition, giving his characters an emotional range that had never been seen in drama to that date.

What this enables Shakespeare to do is create a man who we feel sympathy for throughout the play. This is no easy thing to do: he murders a king and has others murder his best friend and a mother and child - yet at the end we still feel some emotional attachment to him.

Shakespeare achieves this by giving Macbeth the quality of self-reflection - even at the end he questions the meaning of it all.

If you recall something we explored earlier, we can also see Macbeth's character as a vehicle through which Shakespeare is able to explore what happens to a brave and heroic man and his noble wife who disrupt the divine right of kings by murdering Duncan.

The Macbeths' tragic ending is designed to serve as a stark warning to anyone who might consider regicide, which is why King James I was so pleased with the play.

Let's turn now to some of the key elements of Macbeth's character that you might be asked to explore in your exam.

MACBETH AS A BRAVE WARRIOR

There are many references to Macbeth's masculine bravery in the play, particularly in its opening scenes. As we've seen, his strength is impressive: he is able to 'unseam' Macdonwald from 'the nave to th' chops' which would mean him cutting the man open from his belly to his throat. That would take some doing, particularly when you consider the heavy, unwieldy swords these men took into battle.

ACT 1 SCENE 1: THE BATTLE

The Sergeant refers to him as 'brave Macbeth' and 'valour's minion' (literally, 'bravery's favourite' as 'minion' is taken from the French 'mignon'). Duncan then refers to him as his 'valiant cousin', which is high praise indeed. These are important initial references to Macbeth (who we have not yet met) as they paint the picture of a man who has growing status in Scottish society.

Remember: the higher the tragic hero is at the start, the further he has to fall. He has everything to lose by murdering the King - this is what Shakespeare wants us to realise.

BRAVERY AND PRIDE

His former bravery becomes even more important when it is used as a tool against him by his wife. We needed to have seen how fearless a warrior Macbeth has been so that Lady Macbeth can remind him of his manliness and show how not killing Duncan is the coward's way out.

Remember the language she uses in Act 1 Scene 7? How she calls him 'a coward' and how 'when you durst do it, then you were a man'? She's deliberately targeting the most sensitive spot of Macbeth's character - his masculinity.

We can look more at what this tells us about Lady Macbeth a little later, but for now all we need to understand is that both Macbeth's and Shakespeare's times were deeply patriarchal societies (with men holding all positions of power in society and in the family).

Men wore the trousers, so to speak. So for Macbeth's wife to challenge his masculine pride like this would have been close to intolerable. And she knew it.

Towards the end of Act 1 Scene 7, Macbeth's change of heart is reflected in his language:

> *I am settled, and bend up*
> *Each corporal agent to this terrible feat.*

Notice how he uses physical language here - ' each corporal agent' meaning 'every power of his body'. He is a physical man, one who is used to allowing actions to speak louder than words.

Again, this will prove important when he becomes king, as it's not all about how strong you are - there are political elements to leadership that Macbeth seems unsuited to.

A FRAGILE VALOUR - AFTER THE MURDER

In Act 2 Scene 2, when Macbeth comes from Duncan's bedchamber with the bloody daggers still in his hands, he tells his wife that he had heard one of the Grooms cry 'sleep no more'. Lady Macbeth immediately refers back to his physical strength:

> *Why, worthy Thane,*
> *You do unbend your noble strength, to think*
> *So brainsickly of things.*

It's interesting how overthinking could weaken Macbeth: as a man of action, he needs to focus on getting stuff done and not spending too much time pondering right and wrong. At least this is how his wife seems to see him.

When he refuses to go back in to replace the daggers, Lady Macbeth finishes the job. When she returns, her hands bloodied, she says:

> *My hands are of your colour; but I shame*
> *To wear a heart so white.*

She would be ashamed to act in such a cowardly way, being unable to finish what he had started. So why can't he? Why is it that Macbeth can literally slice someone in half on the battle field only a day or so before, and now cannot complete a task that should make him king?

This is one of the reasons we are able to stay with Macbeth throughout the tragic hero's journey. If he had come out of the bedchamber either emotionless or celebrating what he had achieved, we would immediately switch our sympathy off. But he does not. He is already deeply haunted by what he has done. His is a profoundly human reaction, a reaction to trauma.

As I mentioned earlier, Shakespeare was the first playwright to really show human psychology: and this is a very good example. We cannot condone what he has done but we can certainly understand his reaction. This was not something he wanted to do.

GOING DOWN FIGHTING

Macbeth's bravery does not desert him at the end of the play. After his final soliloquy, where he comes to a realisation of the ultimate meaninglessness of life (his *anagnorisis*, remember - his moment of sudden realisation when it's too late to change things), he prepares to fight to the death. Like his profoundly human reaction to the murder of Duncan, these final moments ensure the audience is not totally against Macbeth at the end.

Making audiences care

How often have you seen a movie where you just don't care what happens to any character by the end? Probably more than you can count. This is because the writer and director don't take the time to build up a character with the sorts of flaws and problems that we can relate to.

If a writer creates a sympathetic character at the start, we are far more likely to follow them to the end, regardless of what they do and how much they change.

For a brilliant example of this, watch 'Breaking Bad': the main character starts as a chemistry teacher and ends as a murderous, methamphetamine drug baron, yet we still care what happens to him.

Same with Macbeth: he does terrible things in the play but we are still rooting for him even though we know he deserves to be punished for what he did. These conflicting audience emotions are some of the most powerful, and Shakespeare exploits these brilliantly.

In Act 5 Scene 3, when he hears that the English troops are approaching, he demands that he be readied for battle, saying 'I'll fight till from my bones my flesh be hacked'. Fighting is all he really knows, so it makes sense that he is prepared to focus on what he is best at.

He has failed as king, caused famine and great unhappiness throughout Scotland, his wife's suicide only adding to the hopelessness he feels. Yet he will not lie down and surrender. It's not in his blood and we have to applaud him for that.

MACBETH'S AMBITION

Along with his pride, Macbeth's ambition is his *hamartia* or 'fatal flaw'. It is the quality that has got him to this point in his life, where he is Thane of Glamis and soon to be Thane of Cawdor, with a castle and the respect of his peers. It has driven him to huge success on the battlefield and will now drive him to commit murder to get what he believes he deserves.

THE WITCHES SEWING THE SEEDS IN ACT 1 SCENE 3

We see the seeds of his grander ambitions early in the play. When the witches proclaim 'All hail, Macbeth, that shalt be kind hereafter!' his response shows us that they have touched a nerve. If he had laughed at them or called them ridiculous we might believe that being king had never before crossed his mind.

But when Banquo says 'Good sir, why do you start: and seem to fear / Things that do sound so fair?' we know that he had already considered becoming king through some dishonourable act. He may not have discussed it with his wife, it may have been something deep down inside him, but it's clear that this is something he had considered.

LADY MACBETH SUGGESTS PRIOR DISCUSSION OF THE MURDER PLOT

Although she doesn't out and out say it, there are hints that they had discussed Macbeth's future 'promotion' before the play begins. We can therefore assume that this seed had been growing in Macbeth's head for some time. It's more than likely because of the growing respect he has gained as a fearsome warrior - a vital stepping stone on the way to high status in Scottish society.

If we look again at Act 1 Scene 7, when Macbeth tells his wife that 'we will proceed no further in this business', she uses both 'hope' and 'desire' to argue that his prior words are not being supported by his present actions.

The fact she is so surprised by his about turn suggests that they had discussed the murder in some depth. Certainly, if you look at how Lady Macbeth reacts to Macbeth's letter in Act 1 Scene 5, she is very quick to turn to plotting. This cannot then have been a surprise to her.

What is probably more telling is how Lady Macbeth refers to a previous murder plan that Macbeth had devised. As a warrior, Macbeth is clearly not set out for planning such complexities, which Lady Macbeth refers to mockingly:

> *Nor time nor place*
> *Did then adhere, and yet you would make both*

She is telling him that he was happy to murder Duncan when the time and place weren't right, but now everything is set up perfectly he is backing out.

This shows us that Macbeth had the ambition both to wish to become king and to plan the murder himself, but his lack of the more subtle, scheming qualities needed to make this work meant that his wife had to take over and become the planner.

This is a key element of the tragic hero's *hamartia*: they have some of the qualities needed for success but something is missing. Romeo misses patience - an ability to bite his tongue and bide his time. Othello is unable to be rational and believe that his wife is not guilty of adultery.

Macbeth fails to understand that along with ambition must come higher qualities such as fairness and honour. Without these he is doomed as soon as he enters Duncan's bedchamber.

THE WITCHES AS GARDENERS, WATERING THE SEEDS OF AMBITION

On first reading we might see the witches as supernatural beings who somehow cast a spell on Macbeth and magically turn him into a king. But this is not what happens at all. They actually do nothing other than suggest his future. That really is it: it's like they know the seeds are there, and their job is to add water and watch them grow. They don't plant the seeds in the first place.

Both times - when he first meets them and when he goes back to them later in the play - they suggest his fate, and that of Banquo (which of course is one of the reasons Banquo's life ends badly, because they prophecy that his descendants will be kings). And everything else is up to Macbeth and his wife.

It is as if the prophecies legitimise his desires for kingship: you can almost imagine him thinking 'well, if the weird sisters have said it then it's bound to happen and there's nothing I can do about it'.

Fate

There's a reason for this: unlike today, when we have science and rational arguments and so on, both at the time Shakespeare was writing and at the time the play was set, people genuinely believed in fate: that their lives were mapped out by God and that there wasn't much they could do to alter it.

A lot of this was in place to stop people from rebelling - if you were king then this was because it was God's choice, just like if you were starving in the gutter. You couldn't break out of that cycle because God had decided that that was your position in life. All you could really do was pray that God would give you a break.

It was only really when people began to realise that there was more to life than slavishly following your church, king or master that things began to change. It started almost 200 years after Macbeth, in Paris, culminating in the French revolution of 1789.

But at the time of Macbeth, there was no such questioning. This is why Macbeth takes the word of the witches so literally. As far as he is concerned his fate has already been decided.

MACBETH'S FUNDAMENTAL DECENCY

Of course, when we read the play and see what awful things he does to get and keep power, it's easy to overlook the fact that, when the play starts, Macbeth comes across as a pretty decent guy.

This is important: if he was a monster from the start, a) we wouldn't see the typical downwards trajectory of the tragic hero and b) we wouldn't care about what happens to him. I think Shakespeare is saying that he is not an unusual man, and that this could happen to anyone, given the right set of circumstances. As we've seen, plays like this are full of lessons.

Duncan speaks highly of Macbeth, calling him 'worthiest cousin' for his efforts on the battlefield. But it's Lady Macbeth's judgement of Macbeth in Act 1 Scene 5 that is most telling. As soon as she finishes the letter which tells her of the witches' prophecy and how the first part has already come true, she gives this speech:

> *Glamis thou art, and Cawdor, and shalt be*
> *What thou art promised: yet do I fear thy nature;*
> *It is too full o' the milk of human kindness*
> *To catch the nearest way: thou wouldst be great;*
> *Art not without ambition, but without*
> *The illness should attend it.*

Lady Macbeth is scared that her husband's fundamental goodness will stop him from realising his ambitions. This isn't just a surface thing with Macbeth, it is part of his 'nature'. She recognises that he is ambitious, but doesn't have the 'illness' (the darkness of character) to commit murder in order to become king.

We can also see this in his relationship with his wife. He is a loving husband, respectful of Lady Macbeth and devastated when she dies at the end. This is one of the reasons why we don't reject Macbeth when he commits such awful acts - we can see that he does have some positive qualities.

DECENCY AND SELF-DOUBT

It is this fundamental decency that causes such **self doubt** in Macbeth. From the very start he is not sure whether he should go ahead with the murder: 'He hath honoured me of late; and I have bought / Golden opinions from all sorts of people' (Act 1 Scene 7).

He likes to be liked - it feels good to have so many people speak so well of him. If it wasn't for his wife it would seem certain that he would never go through with it - it's because of his love, respect and (possibly) fear of her that he agrees. That, plus the fact that the witches have said it will happen.

This is why the themes of Macbeth are so eternal: how often do we hear of so-called decent people making the wrong choices out of greed or because they are easily led? We see it in the news all the time, usually linked to politicians. Human nature hasn't changed much in the four hundred or so years since Shakespeare was writing.

This doubt shows itself again at the end of the play in the famous 'Tomorrow' soliloquy: he doubts the meaning of life itself, calling it nothing more than a 'walking shadow'. It is this deep self-reflection that makes Macbeth such a fascinating and flawed character: even in the middle of such drama he is able to take a moment to question it all.

LADY MACBETH

Lady Macbeth is one of Shakespeare's most fascinating characters. Whilst she is only on stage a handful of times, her role in Macbeth's decision-making and ultimate downfall is immense.

She is a cold, cruel and merciless woman whose death at the end of the play as as much to do with her losing power and control as it is any pressure heaped on her through the terrible acts Macbeth commits in order to achieve and sustain their plan.

It's important to understand that Lady Macbeth represents a certain type of Shakespearean woman: strong, assertive, and therefore dangerous. And, like other strong women before her, the narrative will need to punish her, to bring her back in line and under male control.

Women with a voice cannot be allowed to speak without some sort of correction by men. Let's look at why this is.

Marry / go mad / die: Shakespeare's leading ladies

One key convention of Shakespeare's plays is how their leading ladies end up. If we look at his two major forms of drama - the Tragedy and the Comedy - we can see that women are treated in very different ways. The third type of drama he wrote - the History plays - are less clear cut in how both men and women are treated.

In his Comedies (like *Much Ado About Nothing* and *The Taming of the Shrew*) strong women are tamed by the end of the play and end up marrying. Think Beatrice in *Much Ado*, or Katherine in *The Taming of the Shrew*. Even the title of the latter gives the game away - a 'shrew' is a stubborn, strong-willed woman.

In his Tragedies, however, these strong women (such as Ophelia in *Hamlet*, Desdemona in *Othello* and Cordelia in *King Lear*) end up dying. This is because the conventions of the Tragedy don't allow for a happy ending, so the only way these women can be silenced is by their lives ending in some tragic way.

This is often through suicide after a period of madness. In both *Hamlet* and *Macbeth*, Ophelia and Lady Macbeth lose their minds before killing themselves. It is as if they can no longer cope with the pressures placed on them by being a strong woman in a male society, and their minds finally break.

Why did Shakespeare write like this? Was it just because he had a problem with women? Not at all: it was because, at that time, there was an expectation for women to know their place - to stay silent, know who was in charge, not question men or attempt to assert themselves.

For those who did, either they'd be tamed by the man (and be grateful - both Beatrice and Katherine seem much happier when they are married at the end of their plays) or they'd lose their life.

Like the warning 'if you kill a king things will only end bad for you', constantly seeing women being treated like this would have sent a strong message to the female population:

'do as you're told or the same thing could happen to you - marriage will make you happy, rebelling will not.'

It may be tough for a modern audience to see, but this is just how it was at that time.

OUR FIRST IMPRESSIONS OF LADY MACBETH

What is interesting about the first words Lady Macbeth speaks is that they are not her own. She enters in Act 1 Scene 5 reading a letter from Macbeth, in which he tells her of what the witches prophesied and how the first prophecy immediately came true.

This establishes Lady Macbeth as an enabler of her husband: not the main character, but rather someone who enables Macbeth to become king through her words and actions.

If we examine her immediate response to this we gain an insight into her personality before we learn anything more about her:

> *Glamis thou art, and Cawdor; and shalt be*
> *What thou art promised.*

There's no surprise in her tone, no shock at this extraordinary. Cool, calm and calculating: Lady Macbeth has no doubt that Macbeth will be king. This suggests that they'd already been discussing his future; which, based on the forcefulness of her personality, would not be a surprise.

As we've explored before, her fear is Macbeth's ultimate goodness - that he is 'too full o' the milk of human kindness' to be able to act in the way that would realise these ambitions. Fortunately for Macbeth, his wife has none of that goodness:

> *Hie thee hither,*
> *That I may pour my spirits in thine ear;*
> *And chastise with the valour of my tongue*
> *All that impedes thee from the golden round.*

It is the 'valour' of her 'tongue' that is Lady Macbeth's most powerful tool. She is able to talk Macbeth into these crimes, to remove his 'human kindness' and convince him to murder king Duncan. But, as we have just mentioned, women with strong voices have to be silenced and tamed: and we will see this as the play moves on.

HER FIRST SOLILOQUY

We explored Lady Macbeth's opening soliloquy in the summary of the play, but I think it worth looking at it once more with a focus on what we learn about Lady Macbeth's character as she speaks.

What is first apparent is how she refers to the castle: she says 'my battlements', not 'our'. She clearly sees the castle as her own.

However, as a vassal of the king, neither Macbeth nor Lady Macbeth would own any of their property or possessions. *Vassalage* is the term given to the obligations men like Macbeth have towards their king in return for titles, land and property.

The king gives Macbeth the titles of thane of Glamis and then Cawdor, and expects total loyalty and obedience in return.

This small slip of the tongue by Lady Macbeth perhaps suggests that she already sees herself as queen and the castle as her own. Interesting.

> As a quick aside, it is this ability to take a single word and say lots about it that determines whether a candidate will get the highest grades in their exam. If you can focus in on these tiny details and say lots about them you'll be well on the way to a top grade.

Her desire to be 'unsexed' links back to what we mentioned above: she understands that femininity is not a suitable quality to show at this moment, so wants these 'spirits who tend on mortal thoughts' to remove this part of her.

Being female is being weak as far as she is concerned: and she cannot be weak right now.

She continues on the same theme, commanding these spirits to 'take my milk for gall': to turn the thing that gives life into poison. It is the most unique part of being a woman, this ability to feed a child with her own milk. Lady Macbeth wants this to not only be removed, but to made something that can damage life rather than sustain it.

She uses the personal pronoun 'my' once more at the end - it is her reference to 'my keen knife' that is the most interesting, as it suggests that Lady Macbeth herself planned on committing the murder herself (this is backed up when, in Act 2 Scene 2, she says about the murder 'Had he not resembled / My father as he slept, I had done't').

From the moment she speaks, Lady Macbeth is presented as an immensely strong-willed, ambitious and calculating woman, someone who will do whatever it takes to ensure her husband achieves what she firmly believes is his right.

Nothing will get in the way of the plan, and she is prepared to strip away any last remaining element of her femininity in order to achieve it.

HER RELATIONSHIP WITH MACBETH

From the moment they meet, we sense that Lady Macbeth is 'in charge'. When Macbeth tells her that Duncan is arriving that night, her response is chilling:

> *O, never*
> *Shall sun that morrow see!*

When Macbeth clearly expresses surprise at the suddenness of the murder plan, Lady Macbeth tells him to hide his emotions:

> *Your face, my thane, is as a book where men*
> *May read strange matters…*
> *…Look like the innocent flower,*
> *But be the serpent under't.*

She spends much of their time together in these opening scenes directing him how to look, how to act, and how to speak. It is almost as if she is speaking to a child who does not understand how things work. It's also interesting that she uses a feminine metaphor for innocence - the 'flower'. At this point in the play the male/female roles seem firmly reversed.

This sense of her taking charge of the plot is reinforced at the end of Act 1 Scene 5, when she commands him to 'Look up clear' (maintain a clear, guiltless expression) and 'Leave all the rest to me'. She will do everything: all he has to do is to look innocent.

THE FLOWER AND SERPENT IN ACTION

We see how good Lady Macbeth is at hiding her true intentions when Duncan arrives. In Act 1 Scene 6 she is the gracious hostess, welcoming the king and heaping praises on him.

Because we know what is about to happen, these words seem even more poisonous: it is as if she is mocking him, putting on an act yet all the while preparing to end his life.

This theme continues throughout the first part of the play: the single most important quality she wishes her passionate, emotional husband to have is this ability to hide his emotions. Without this all is ruined.

Lady Macbeth continues to act well into Act 2 Scene 3, when Duncan's body is discovered. She is clearly shocked at what has happened, so much so that she feints. She is able to use the expected female reaction to remove herself from the scene: very convenient.

'WAS THE HOPE DRUNK?': LADY MACBETH IN ACT 1 SCENE 7

Between Act 1 Scenes 5 and 7 Macbeth has had a change of mind. Duncan has arrived, people have been saying nice things about him, and he is definitely 'feeling the love'. He tells his wife 'We will proceed no further in this business' which of course is not what the uber-ambitious and utterly determined Lady Macbeth wants to hear.

As we explored earlier, she uses the most powerful tool in her weaponry in order to convince Macbeth to do it. This takes us once more back to the opening points in this chapter: it is the delineation between male and female that Lady Macbeth subverts from the moment she opens her mouth.

To her, being masculine is about being decisive, focused and without emotion. Look at the language she uses when she tells Macbeth to sort himself out: is his hope 'drunk'? Does it now wake 'green and pale'? Is he 'afeard' and a 'coward'?

She tells him his mind is not clear, that his emotions have clouded his judgement and made him weak. She needs him to *man up*, in fact. (Awful expression but seems appropriate in this context.)

She pointedly questions his masculinity: 'When you durst do it, then you were a man'. As far as she is concerned, he will not truly be a man until he commits the act of murder. She has so convinced herself that this is the only way forward that anything that gets in her way has to be dealt with, even if it's her husband.

She is disgusted by his change of heart and uses the most important weapon she has, assaulting his masculine pride.

LADY MACBETH HAD A CHILD

Another thing we learn through this dialogue is the fact that Lady Macbeth once had a child:

> *I have given suck, and know*

How tender 'tis the child that milks me.

Perhaps this is one of the reasons she has become so hard and cruel? Not having children has made her focus on herself and her husband's wishes and desires, as there has been no one else to take her mind off herself.

Having lost a child might also have had a profound impact on Lady Macbeth's character. We don't know for sure, but this inability to have a family may have removed some of her more nurturing characteristics.

It's important not to make excuses for her terrible behaviour, but it is interesting to consider what might have led Lady Macbeth to act in the way she does.

THE DANGER OF OVERTHINKING: AFTER THE MURDER

Lady Macbeth is someone who prefers action to thought. She dislikes Macbeth's hesitancy before the murder, and is even more unimpressed at his state of mind as he leaves the bedchamber having murdered the king.

In Act 2 Scene 2, as Macbeth rants about not being able to say 'Amen' when the grooms said 'God bless us', Lady Macbeth's reply is 'Consider it no so deeply':

> *These deeds must not be thought*
> *After these ways; so, it will make us mad.*

She wants Macbeth to do the deed and move on, to get over it quickly as there are other things to consider. She knows that if he spends too much time thinking over what he has done it could make them both mad. This is ironic of course as Lady Macbeth does indeed lose her mind. It is not because she overthinks, however.

For Lady Macbeth, two murders therefore need to take place: both the physical act of killing, but also the death of Macbeth's emotions.

She needs him to become machinelike: without this they are both doomed to fail.

A REVERSAL OF ROLES: ACT 3 SCENE 2

No sooner does Macbeth become king then Lady Macbeth ceases to be of much use. We notice this at the start of Act 3 Scene 2: Lady Macbeth finds her husband alone and brooding. She is obviously fearful of the fact that Banquo is still alive:

> *Nought's had, all's spent,*
> *Where our desire is got without content:*
> *'Tis safer to be that which we destroy*
> *Than by destruction dwell in doubtful joy.*

They have achieved their desire but it is meaningless if this joy is doubtful because there are still loose ends (aka Banquo) to be tied up (aka he needs to be removed from the picture).

However, what is interesting is how Macbeth responds when she asks him 'what's to be done?' over the Banquo and Fleance problem:

> *Be innocent of the knowledge, dearest chuck,*
> *Till thou applaud the deed.*

For the first time, he is planning things without her input. Note how he refers to her as 'dearest chuck'- a term of endearment but not one that presents her as the fearless, cold and calculating woman we have come to expect.

She is no longer in control; now that Macbeth has become king he no longer needs her to plan for him. He has found an inner hardness that has enabled him to commit these acts without her support.

Notice that Shakespeare does not allow her to respond: Macbeth ends the scene with a similar incantation to that spoken by Lady Macbeth in Act 1 Scene 5. Lady Macbeth is now without voice - the one thing she had that offered her control over her fate and that of her husband.

THE CONTROL SLIPS FURTHER: ACT 3 SCENE 4

The banquet scene shows Lady Macbeth having lost any control of her husband. Macbeth sees the ghost of Banquo and attempts to use the same approach that has worked before:

> *Are you a man?...*
> *...these flaws and starts,*
> *Imposters to true fear, would well become*
> *A woman's story at a winter's fire...*
> *...What, quite unmann'd in folly?*

However, trying to belittle his masculinity is no longer effective: he is too far removed from the scene, caught within the terrifying vision he sees, to pay any attention to her.

Once she has removed the guests from the banqueting hall, and is alone with Macbeth, we get a sense of weary resignation from her. She is tired, unsure how to stop everything unravelling. When Macbeth asks 'What is the night?' she replies 'Almost at odds with morning, which is which.'

She no longer knows night from day, right from wrong. It is from this moment that we will see Lady Macbeth unravelling, and will next see her when she sleepwalks the castle at night, betraying her guilty secrets to the Doctor and Gentlewoman.

LADY MACBETH'S MADNESS: ACT 5 SCENE 1

We've already looked a little at this scene, but it's worth spending time looking at it more closely in the light of what we explored earlier in this section about why Lady Macbeth loses her mind.

Remember: rebellious women are either married (comedies) or die (tragedies) by the end of the play. It's true that the tragic hero also dies, but this is a heroic death, one filled with drama and poetry, where the audience see the hero's true qualities before his final downfall.

Not so with Lady Macbeth (or Ophelia in Hamlet). The moments before her death are rather pathetic. She speaks hurriedly, disjointedly, her hands rubbing together as she asks 'will these hands ne'er be clean?' She seems at times to be addressing Macbeth - ' Wash your hands, put on your nightgown' - and at times to be speaking to herself:

> *All the*
> *Perfumes of Arabia will not sweeten this little*
> *hand. Oh, oh, oh!*

The scene very much centres on Lady Macbeth's hands: even though she committed no murders herself she has both literal and metaphorical blood on her hands. Her tortured sleepwalking is the manifestation of the guilt she now feels. It is as if her mind can no longer hold such dreadful secrets and has to let them out.

But why does Shakespeare show this scene before her suicide? For the same reason why he shows Macbeth reflecting on the meaningless of life before his final battle. If neither character showed this vulnerability we would not identify with their pain and struggle.

If Lady Macbeth had gone from being a controlling mastermind to jumping from the window without this final scene, we would have cared little. However, because we see her in this vulnerable state we care far more.

There is one other reason why Shakespeare shows this profound anxiety and trauma, and it is one we have already explored.

Remember how we looked at this play as a warning to others not to go around killing kings? Well, here is another classic example. We even have the doctor making sure the audience is one hundred percent clear on the message:

> *Unnatural deeds*
> *Do breed unnatural troubles: infected minds*
> *To their deaf pillows will discharge their secrets.*

By going against the laws of nature in murdering a king, Lady Macbeth's mind has become infected. Let that be a lesson to you, audience - if you decide to commit regicide you may as well say goodbye to your sanity.

BANQUO

Like most tragedies, the other characters in *Macbeth* play a far smaller role than the tragic hero and heroine. However, it is worth spending a little time on each of them in order to understand what they add to the character of Macbeth and his wife.

BANQUO THE WARRIOR

Macbeth is not the only one who comes out of the battle at the start of the play with a positive report. In Act 1 Scene 2, Macbeth and Banquo are presented as heroic, fearless warriors:

> *As cannons overcharged with double cracks, so they*
> *Doubly redoubled strokes upon the foe.*

Interestingly, it is Macbeth who will be rewarded with a new title as a result of his deeds in battle and not Banquo. This suggests that, from the start, Banquo is very much second to Macbeth, more follower than leader.

BANQUO AS AN OPEN BOOK

When Macbeth and Banquo meet the Witches in Act 1 Scene 3, what is noticeable is how much more Banquo speaks. From the moment they see the three women Banquo is an open book about his feelings, contrasting with Macbeth who initially says little. When the Witches hail Macbeth as thane of Glamis, Cawdor and as 'king hereafter', Banquo is the one who responds:

> *Good sir, why do you start and seem to fear*
> *Things that do sound so fair? I' the name of truth,*
> *Are ye fantastical, or that indeed*
> *Which outwardly ye show? My noble partner*
> *You greet with present grace and great prediction*
> *Of noble having and of royal hope*
> *That he seems rapt withal.*

Of course, Banquo does not know the reason why Macbeth stands there speechless. Being told that you will be king in future must seem 'fair' indeed to Banquo, because he has no idea that Macbeth has been thinking about this for some time. We learn here that there is no devious, calculating side to Banquo: he is a good man, honourable and with a clear conscience.

This is why he acts in such an open way, speaking his thoughts without worry as to how they may sound. He is curious as to what the Witches might say about his future:

> *If you can look into the seeds of time,*
> *And say which grain will grow and which may not,*
> *Speak then to me, who neither beg nor fear*
> *Your favours nor your hate.*

This sums Banquo up well - he asks for neither fear nor favours. He is who he is and is respected as a result.

BANQUO AS A HIGHLY RESPECTED NOBLEMAN

We know that Duncan thinks highly of him - in Act 1 Scene 4 he thanks Banquo equally for his services:

> *Noble Banquo,*
> *Thou hast no less deserved, nor must be known*
> *No less to have done so, let me enfold thee*
> *And hold thee to my heart.*

Shakespeare sets Banquo up in this way so that, when Macbeth decides that he and his son should be murdered, the audience is shocked that Macbeth could commit such a terrible act on such a fundamentally good person.

In many ways Banquo acts as a **foil** to the Macbeths' calculated plans for Scottish domination: his essential goodness highlights how low Macbeth and his wife are prepared to go to achieve their ambitions.

The foil: a key dramatic character

Let's take a moment to talk about what we mean by a foil. In essence, *a foil is a character whose purpose is to contrast with the main character in order that the audience learn more about the hero's character and motivations.*

For a fundamentally good hero, the foil might be more sinister: an example being Iago in *Othello*. For someone more complex, such as Macbeth, having a foil like Banquo shows us how Macbeth is changing - as Banquo does not.

THE FUNCTION OF BANQUO'S GHOST

Why does Shakespeare use ghosts in a number of his plays? Further examples include *Hamlet* (where Hamlet's father appears to inform

Hamlet of the circumstances of his death), *Richard III* (where the spirits of Richard's many victims are paraded before him) and *Julius Caesar* (which has the ghost of Julius Caesar appearing before Brutus on the eve of a battle).

The most obvious reason that Shakespeare brings Banquo back on stage is a manifestation of the terrible guilt Macbeth now feels at having murdered his closest friend. This certainly links to the ghosts in both *Richard III* and *Julius Caesar* but perhaps less so in *Hamlet*: the latter serves to tell Hamlet that his own uncle was responsible for regicide.

Many believed that ghosts were spirits who were resting in purgatory, the state between heaven and hell that formed part of the Catholic religious doctrine. Tormented by the circumstances of their death, they come back to haunt the accused, punishing them for their acts.

This is certainly the case in Macbeth, who is the only person to see Banquo: not even Lady Macbeth can see the ghost, such is the sole responsibility that Macbeth must take for Banquo's death.

It also serves to show the audience that Macbeth's until now secret crimes are becoming public: for the first time, Macbeth shows a form of madness in front of the people he is supposed to be ruling.

This is deeply embarrassing for Lady Macbeth and indeed Macbeth himself. Perhaps innocent in life, Banquo's ghost exerts revenge on his killer in death.

From a drama point of view, it also makes for a very powerful scene!

THE WITCHES

They may only appear in three scenes of the play, but their role in the crowning and eventual downfall of Macbeth is vital. It is they who tell him he will be thane of Cawdor and king, and who fill him with false confidence later in the play.

THE SOURCE OF THE WITCHES

The source of Shakespeare's witches lies with Holinshed: in his chronicles he does indeed mention 'creatures of the elder-wood….nymphs or faeries' (Holinshed's Chronicles 286).

If they sound very different from Shakespeare's witches then that's because they are: Holinshed makes no mention of ugly hags with 'skinny lips'. Instead, his sound much more like young, attractive women.

It's no surprise why Shakespeare makes the changes he does. Macbeth meeting three attractive fairies at the start of the play would have far less dramatic impact: because of the nature of his and his wife's evil plans, it's important that the seed for these be planted by more conventionally evil-looking witches.

Remember that, at the time, a belief in witches and their link to the devil was very real.

Another difference with Macbeth is that Shakespeare has Macbeth going back to the witches to learn what will happen next. This does not happen in Holinshed.

Again, we can understand why he'd want to do that - to maintain the supernatural element to the play, to bring in a dramatic scene at the point when the action starts to lessen, to fill Macbeth with the false confidence he needs to carry him through to the end of the play - that second visit is an effective dramatic technique.

THE ROLE OF THE WITCHES

As we mentioned in the scene by scene summary, the original name for the witches was 'wyrd sisters' - and, according to the Oxford English Dictionary, 'wyrd' is old Anglo Saxon for 'the principal, power, or agency by which events are predetermined; fate, destiny'.

This is interesting when applied to the Witches' role in the play. We could say that the Witches do have this power to predetermine events, to look into the future and (in Banquo's words) to 'say which grain will grow and which will not'.

However, what we need to be careful of is seeing them as somehow casting a spell over Macbeth, filling him with the evil he needs to commit the terrible acts later in the play.

They do not: it is Lady Macbeth who spurs him on to murder king Duncan: all the Witches do is tell him that he will be king. Lady Macbeth commands the 'spirits who tend on mortal thoughts' to 'fill her' full of 'direst cruelty'. The three Witches are not responsible for this.

The Witches' role is twofold: firstly, they have been created by Shakespeare to add to the sinister, supernatural feel to the play. The audience of the time would have shuddered to see such dreadful women helping Macbeth on his way to power and ultimate doom.

Secondly, they make public what Macbeth and his wife had clearly been thinking about before the play begins. They provide the final motivation for the murders to be committed.

Any drama has to have an *inciting event*: something that happens to the main character that starts the storyline off. Macbeth may have been considering becoming king, and his ambitious wife had certainly thought about it in the past, but until the Witches plant that seed it was nothing more than thoughts.

The Witches' main role therefore is *catalyst*: they are responsible for starting Macbeth off on his journey without actually doing anything themselves.

MACDUFF

Whilst he is only in a handful of scenes, Macduff's role in the play is pivotal. We have referred to Banquo as a foil to Macbeth, highlighting our tragic hero's faults through his own goodness. The same can be said for Macduff, but probably more so.

MACDUFF THE AVENGING, HOLY WARRIOR

In many ways Macduff can be seen as an avenger, helping Malcolm to reclaim Scotland from the tyranny of Macbeth's rule. He begins the play with the same status as Macbeth (he is thane of Fife) and remains close to Duncan's son Malcolm, leaving Scotland to persuade Malcolm to return with the English army to defeat Macbeth.

On the way he loses his wife and children, murdered by Macbeth in a drive to ensure that Macduff's children do not become king.

Macduff is presented as a holy warrior, driven by a high moral purpose, unlike Macbeth who is only interested in his own greed and self-satisfaction. In this way he represents the perfect foil to Macbeth, emphasising good moral leadership over tyranny.

In Act 3 Scene 6, when Lennox and a Lord 'fill in the blanks' between the action, the Lord mentions that Macduff:

> *Is gone to pray the holy king, upon his aid*
> *To wake Northumberland and warlike Siward,*
> *That, by the help of these - with Him above*
> *To ratify the work - we may again*
> *Give to our tables meat, sleep to our nights.*

He and Siward are sanctioned by 'Him above', meaning that they have God on their side. Lennox refers to Macduff as 'some holy angel'. It is clear that Shakespeare is setting good against evil: the faithful servant of the true king against the unwelcome and despised current king.

We further see Macduff's innate goodness when he speaks to Malcolm just before he learns of his wife and children's murder.

In Act 4 Scene 3 Malcolm gives the rather odd speech to Macduff in which he admits to being selfish, greedy, lustful and not fit to be king. Macduff's pained response - 'O Scotland, Scotland!' - is just what Malcolm needs to hear: Macduff has passed the test of loyalty and proven his honour.

REACTING TO HIS FAMILY'S MURDER

Where we see the biggest contrast between the two 'Macs' is in their reaction to their wive's deaths. When Macduff hears of his family's death his reaction is one of extreme anguish: when Malcolm tells Macduff to 'dispute it like a man', Macduff replies 'I must also feel it as a man'. For Macduff, showing pain is not something to be ashamed of.

He shows a humanity that is sadly lacking in Macbeth. We see this in Act 5 Scene 5 when the doctor informs Macbeth of Lady Macbeth's death: his response - 'she should have died hereafter / There would have been time for such a word' - is in comparison cold and detached.

Macduff cannot believe that his family has been taken from him: Macbeth seems resigned to it. He does not believe his wife should have died so young, but recognises the inevitability of death. There is a beauty in his following soliloquy but also a coldness to it.

MACDUFF'S MORALITY

Macduff leaves his family in order to persuade Malcolm to return and fight for the Scottish crown. In so doing he leaves them vulnerable to attack. Lady Macduff is unhappy about his decision: 'His flight was madness' she says to Ross.

Nonetheless, Macduff seems bound by a moral purpose which causes him to take this risk. What is sad is that Lady Macduff and her son die feeling anger and bitterness towards Macduff: he has sacrificed much in order to remove Macbeth from the throne.

OTHER CHARACTERS

KING DUNCAN

The character of King Duncan is taken from Holinshed's Chronicles. However, unlike the weak, incompetent king Holinshed writes about, Shakespeare's Duncan is a noble, strong and deeply respected man. He is the father-figure whose removal from the throne disrupts the natural order of Scotland, in the way that a father leaving his family would disrupt the family's equilibrium in profound ways.

As we've seen before, in Shakespeare's England the king is believed to have a direct link to God, so removing him in such a violent way is bound to cause far-reaching problems, both within society and within nature itself.

His death at the start of the play is what starts Scotland's descent into chaos. It is only through Macbeth's death that order can be restored at the end.

Duncan is a noble, fair man, but exerts powerful rule when need be. At the start of the play he passes the sentence of death on the thane of Cawdor:

> *No more that Thane of Cawdor shall deceive*
> *Our bosom interest. Go pronounce his present death*
> *And with his former title greet Macbeth.*

In contrast, he shows a sensitivity when he arrives at the Macbeths' castle:

> *This castle hath a pleasant seat. The air*
> *Nimbly and sweetly recommends itself*
> *Unto our gentle senses.*

Some might argue that Duncan shows naivety in believing that Macbeth has no suspicious intentions, but then again Macbeth has demonstrated total bravery and loyalty on the battlefield so why should the king believe that the new thane of Cawdor is anything other than faithful?

Even though Duncan is only in the play in Act 1 his role is vital, as he represents order: the strength of his rule, his fairness, the love his subjects have for him: through his removal Scotland is thrown into anarchy, with disastrous results for its people.

MALCOLM

Malcolm is the eldest son of King Duncan and the heir to his throne. After Duncan is murdered, Malcolm flees for England: his younger brother Donalbain heads to Ireland. From his English base he and the English King Siward assemble troops to remove Macbeth from power.

In many ways Malcolm represents order and good moral leadership. Whilst he is less of a foil to Macbeth, he nonetheless shows the audience how to act in a patient, measured way in order to achieve his goal.

In this respect he is like his father Duncan before him: a good king, who has his people's best interests at heart rather than being motivated by greed and self-interest.

Malcolm's key scene comes in Act 4 Scene 3. He shows a measured, thoughtful approach to the pain he feels at Macbeth's rule:

> *What I believe I'll wail,*
> *What know believe, and what I can redress,*
> *As shall find the time to friend, I will.*

There is no rushing to judgment and an understanding that where he can make a difference, he will. This is in marked contrast to Macbeth's irrational belief in the impossibility of the Witches' prophecies coming true and his hot-blooded temperament.

Malcolm comes across as the thoughtful politician rather than the passionate tyrant.

His testing of Macduff shows a steelier nature. He tells Macduff that he is a lustful, violent man who does not deserve to be king:

> *…there's no bottom, none,*
> *In my voluptuousness: your wives, your daughters,*
> *Your matrons and your maids, could not fill up*
> *The cistern of my lust.*

He goes on in a similar way until Macduff cries 'O Scotland, Scotland!':

> *Fit to govern!*
> *No, not fit to live.*

Malcolm draws out of Macduff precisely the reaction he needed in order to ensure the latter is fully on his side. It is a clever, political move that shows Malcolm's approach to leadership.

In the final moments of the play, when Macbeth has been killed by Macduff, we again see this calm, almost clinical approach to leadership. He may be acting in this way in deliberate contrast to Macbeth, or this may simply be his character.

He will make his thanes Earls, will call home all those in exile:

> *...and what needful else*
> *That calls upon us, by grace of Grace,*
> *We will perform in measure, time and place*

Everything will happen at the right time and in the right place. It must have been music to the ears of all those hearing him.

THE THEMES

WHAT ARE THEMES?

Put simply, a theme is a big idea about the world explored by the writer. Themes are universal, explored through lots of different novels and plays. They often reflect the time in which the writer is writing.

For example, at the time of Macbeth, there had been many years of instability both in politics and in the royal family. Elizabeth had ruled for many years but there had been numerous attempts to remove her. Catholics and Protestants had been violently opposed to one another since Henry VIII had created the Church of England way back in the 1530s.

Out of this came plays which dealt with the consequences of unstable royal families. Richard III, Macbeth, Hamlet and King Lear all deal with what happens when the natural order of things (the king in absolute and unquestionable power) is disrupted.

Whilst there are numerous smaller themes in Macbeth, they can be broadly broken down as follows. These are a few that may well come up in an exam:

- Paradox and equivocation (don't worry, I'll explain what

these mean in the next section). Within the theme of paradox there are several sub themes, such as appearance and reality
- Ambition
- Masculinity and Femininity

We'll now examine each of these in turn. In a following section we'll focus on how we might answer a theme-based question in the exam.

PARADOX AND EQUIVOCATION

Before we explore this theme, it's probably worth explaining what these two terms mean. If you refer to these more complex ideas (and show you understand them of course) you'll be well on the way to getting the top grades. Examiners like to see candidates use sophisticated terms like this, providing you always explain their effect.

> This is an important point (and one I do go on about quite a lot). Never drop in terms like paradox or metaphor or alliteration unless you show the effect they have on the audience or reader.
>
> Technique spotting is easy and might get you a grade 5. Showing **effect** (in other words **analysing**) is what gets you into the 6s, 7s and beyond…

A *paradox* is a contradiction: more specifically, a statement that contradicts itself. An example would be 'This statement is false'. If it's true that the statement is false then the statement itself cannot be false. Get it? Make your head hurt? It's supposed to. What it does is point to the challenge that language has to pin down the complexities of existence.

Equivocation is using ambiguous language in order to conceal the truth and avoid committing oneself to one point of view or another. Equivocal literally means 'with equal voice'.

In other words, using vague words to hide how you're really feeling, try to conceal the truth, or not commit to one point of view.

Politicians use this sort of language all the time (often beginning an equivocation by saying 'let me be perfectly clear…'). They do this because they don't want to be seen to admit the truth. It can be quite frustrating to watch a politician on a tv news show! They never seem to say anything…

On the other hand, if you say something *unequivocally* you are speaking clearly and with absolute certainty.

Why explore both terms together? Because in combination they create an atmosphere of unease and confusion. When language is both one thing and another, and when characters hide the truth from one another (and often from themselves), no one is sure who is right and who is wrong.

This is what makes Macbeth such a fascinating play: you can never wholly side with one character or another.

PARADOX IN *MACBETH*

Fair and foul

From the opening scene, we are introduced to a world where nothing is as it seems. The language the witches use is filled with paradox: the battle is both 'lost and won', and the weather both 'fair' and 'foul'.

Whilst this creates a mood of uncertainty, both statements also point to a deeper understanding of the subjective nature of reality: if you are in a fight and end up on the floor you've lost, but the other person has won. Same fight, different outcome. Subjective, see?

So battles are indeed lost and won, and one person's fair weather is another person's foul weather. I love hot sunny days, my wife doesn't. Neither of us are right or wrong. It's just a matter of opinion.

Macbeth repeats this 'foul and fair' paradox on entering Act 1 Scene 3: the day is foul because of the storm the Witches have whipped up, and fair because of the recent victory in battle.

It shows us how far Shakespeare is able to move into the depths of the human mind: characters are able to hold two opposing/conflicting emotions at the same time - the positive feelings that come from victory and the negative feelings towards the weather.

Comfort and discomfort

In Act 1 Scene 2, the Sergeant explains to Duncan what happened in the battle. MacDonwald was previously loyal to Duncan but turned traitor. He says to Duncan '...from that spring whence comfort seem'd to come / Discomfort swells.'

From the comfort Duncan should have had in having such a loyal thane in his command, a traitor was born. This foreshadows Macbeth's treachery: Macbeth uses his position close to the king in order to murder him and steal his throne.

For Duncan, the defeat of Macdonwald and the Norwegian king should be cause for great celebration: little does he know what is around the corner. Within victory are the seeds for the most profound of defeats. A paradox indeed!

Lesser, greater, not so happy, happier...

The Witches are masters (mistresses?) of disorder, and use their paradoxical language to create confusion and uncertainty. In Act 1 Scene 3, after the Witches tell Macbeth that he will be king, Banquo asks them to tell him his future:

> *First Witch: Lesser than Macbeth, and greater.*
> *Second Witch: Not so happy, yet much happier.*
> *Third Witch: Thou shalt get kings, though thou be none.*

What do they mean? Well, first of all, they are trying to confuse, to sow seeds of doubt in both Macbeth and Banquo, to get them guessing. Remember, they actually do nothing to alter the course of events - they drop hints, and confusing ones at that. The rest is up to Macbeth and his wife.

We can guess that the Witches are referring to Banquo being lesser in status than Macbeth, but greater in character. However, what is a little confusing (and scholars have been debating this for years) is why Banquo should be unhappy at this point in the play.

He and Macbeth are victorious in battle and are going home to what they must know will be some sort of reward. Perhaps the witches are foreshadowing what will happen to Banquo? His death will be unhappy yet he will die an honourable man, unlike Macbeth who dies shamed and hated. Possibly. Don't let it worry you too much.

Foreshadowing - when events/words earlier in the play hint at what might happen later. So when they do happen we can look back and see the words as being ironic - loaded with meaning.

Ill and good

In Act 1 Scene 3, when the Witches tell Macbeth his prophecy, his aside gives an important insight into both his character and the effect the Witches have had on him:

> *This supernatural soliciting*
> *Cannot be ill, cannot be good.*

Whilst knowing that he will be king has to be a good thing, he also understand that the journey to get there will not be good at all. He immediately recognises the fact that he will have to commit a terrible act in order to achieve his goal.

Caught within his vision of an ideal future is a far from ideal series of steps that have to be taken. This paradox will cause him great anguish, resulting in the 'air drawn dagger' and his growing insomnia.

Appearance and reality

You may well have explored this one in class as it's one that many teachers foreground when teaching themes. Whilst it is important, it's better to see it within the broader theme of paradox.

Lady Macbeth consistently tells Macbeth to hide his true feelings. 'Look like the innocent flower, / But be the serpent under't' she tells Macbeth in Act 1 Scene 5: look innocent, but in actual fact be a snake.

Whilst she finds this relatively easy to do (until the truth comes out in her sleep), Macbeth struggles. He is a passionate warrior not a politician, and Lady Macbeth is worried that he will not be able to remain poker-faced when it matters:

> *Your face, my thane,*
> *Is a book where men may read strange matters.' (Act 1,*
>   *Scene 5)*

In order for the couple to be successful, Macbeth has to hide the reality of his feelings from the outside world. He has to remain calm on the surface. By referring to his face as a 'book', she is reminding him of how important it is to conceal his emotions so that no one can read his true intentions.

This theme is most obviously shown in Act 1 Scene 6, when Duncan comments that the Macbeths' castle

> *hath a pleasant seat; the air*
> *Nimbly and sweetly recommends itself*
> *Unto our gentle senses.*

Of course as an audience we are saying to ourselves 'you have no idea what is about to happen to you, you naive old man!' And that is one of the big benefits of loading the play with these sorts of ironic comments - when we know the reality behind the appearance, we have more information than the characters on stage.

It's a bit like when you went to a pantomime as a kid - you'd be shouting 'look behind you!' when you saw the villain approaching the hero. The same sort of thing is happening here.

Probably the most famous appearance and reality line in the entire play comes at the moment before Macbeth commits the murder:

> *I am settled, and bend up*
> *Each corporal agent to this terrible feat.*
> *Away, and mock the time with fairest show:*
> *False face must hide what the false heart doth know. (Act 1 Scene 7)*

Finally he gets it! It takes him a while for him to understand that he has to hide the truth from everyone if he is going to go through with this. It's interesting that he uses the word 'mock' instead of 'pass'. It's as if he is mocking, or making fun of time itself.

Or it could be the other meaning of 'mock', as in 'fake' (you know, like those mock exams that are probably coming up soon). I think you can read it either way (and examiners love it when you explore possible interpretations, by the way…)

EQUIVOCATION IN MACBETH

The Porter's Speech

Act 2 Scene 3 begins with the Porter's famous monologue, in which he introduces the idea of the 'equivocator'. He makes reference to a 'great equivocator': this is Father Henry Garnet, a Jesuit priest.

Garnet was part of the Gunpowder Plot with Guy Fawkes - their plan was to blow up the Houses of Parliament (for more detail see the section on Context).

Garnet had originally denied being part of it, then changed his mind, saying that his original lies were for God's sake. He was eventually executed by hanging, so his clever words didn't help him one bit.

As we've mentioned before, this play is very clear in its support of the King. There is a warning here: if you lie, or try to hide behind clever language, you will be found out and you will be punished.

Act 2 Scene 3 continues with the Porter explaining to Macduff why drink is an equivocator:

> ...*drink may be said to be an equivocator with lechery: it makes him, and it mars him; it sets him on, and it takes him off; it persuades him, and disheartens him; makes him stand to, and not stand to; in conclusion, equivocates him in a sleep, and, giving him the lie, leaves him.*

He is using vulgar language here - basically, that drink makes a man want sex but stops him from performing. Whilst this scene has been included by Shakespeare as 'comic relief' (inserted into the play to give the audience a breather after Duncan's dramatic murder), Shakespeare has chosen this speech because it resonates with so much of the rest of the play.

Look at the contrasting words: make/mar, on/off, persuades/disheartens, stand to/not stand to. The play is shot through with these constant contrasts, and the effect on the audience is to make them feel constantly uneasy. Even the comic character is in on it.

The Witches' language

The Witches' language is full of equivocation - it is deliberately designed to confuse and mislead. From their very opening 'fair is foul and foul is fair' they sew seeds of confusion wherever they go.

We've seen above the effect that this language has on Macbeth and Banquo when they tell Banquo he is both lesser and greater than

Macbeth. They do the same later in the play when they tell Macbeth he will remain king unless three highly unlikely events happen.

Their final prophecy, that 'none of woman born will harm Macbeth' (Act 4 Scene 1) is highly misleading: Macbeth believes that every man is born of woman so who could possible harm him? This is what gives him such confidence at the end - he feels invincible.

But of course it is the 'born' bit that is misleading - Macduff will tell Macbeth, just before he chops off his head that 'Macduff was from his mother's womb untimely ripp'd' (Act 5 Scene 8): Macduff was born by caesarian section, not in the conventional way. Got you, Macbeth!

Ross conceals the truth from Macduff

We've all done it at some point: told a bit of a white lie to spare someone's feelings. Ross takes this to the extreme in his equivocal language when Macduff asks him how his wife is:

> *Macduff: How does my wife?*
> *Ross: Why, well.*
> *Macduff: And all my children?*
> *Ross: Well, too.*
> *Macduff: The tyrant has not batter'd at their peace?*
> *Ross: No; they were well at peace when I leave them. (Act 4, Scene 3)*

Why does Ross do this? Surely he will have to tell Macduff soon enough that Macbeth has murdered his wife and children. They are 'well', but he means 'well at peace', which is another way of saying dead.

Seems odd to play with language when such a serious thing is being discussed, but this shows that it's not only Macbeth that can conceal the truth through language.

AMBITION

Macbeth is ambitious: we see that from the very opening. No sooner has Ross confirmed the first of the Witches' prophecies by making him Thane of Cawdor, Macbeth is immediately thinking of the future:

> *Glamis, and Thane of Cawdor:*
> *The greatest is behind. (Act 1 Scene 3).*

Whilst he wonders whether it will just be 'chance' that may crown him (line 151) and that 'come what come may' time goes on (line 156), he cannot help but have his ambitions increased through this news.

This is noticeable when Duncan announces Malcolm as next in line to the throne (Act 1 Scene 4). Macbeth realises he is a 'step/ o'er which I must fall down, or else oe'rleap.' (Act Scene 4).

If he is to be successful, Macbeth will have to somehow remove Malcolm as an obstacle. He is already thinking ahead, planning and plotting, which is a clear sign of his ambitious nature.

LADY MACBETH'S GREAT AMBITION

Of course, the most ambitious of all, at least at first, is Lady Macbeth. In Act 1 Scene 5 she clearly indicates what should be done by Macbeth in order to fulfil her ambitions. Murder the king. Nothing could be simpler!

However, she fears that her husband 'Art not without ambition, but without / The illness should attend it.' She knows her husband is ambitious, but in order to get what she believes they deserve, Macbeth must have an 'illness' inside him: must have the qualities a cold-blooded murderer. Without this they will fail.

She wants him beside her so that she can 'pour my spirits in thine ear' - fill him with the cruelty he will need in order to achieve these great ambitions. For Lady Macbeth, the greatest prize - being King and Queen - will require the greatest commitment to an unswerving murderousness.

As we've already seen, Lady Macbeth has to rid herself of anything feminine in order to fulfil her ambitions. Shakespeare seems here to be saying that being ambitious is an inherently male thing: that women cannot have these sorts of characteristics.

At the time the play was written (and indeed until about one hundred years or so ago), women's lives were tightly controlled: they had few if any opportunities for pursuing their own ambitions. They were daughters, then wives, then mothers. That was about it. No need for ambition when you went from one role to another without question.

So, for Lady Macbeth to be ambitious she has to become male. In some ways this links to a quote attributed to Queen Elizabeth I (who ruled England just before the play was written):

> *I know I have but the body of a weak and feeble woman, but I have the heart and stomach of a king, and of a king of England too.*

Elizabeth I also said 'Men fight wars. Women win them.' But that's probably for another time.

MACBETH QUESTIONS WHETHER AMBITION IS ENOUGH

In Act 1 Scene 7, Macbeth is confronted by the dagger. During is soliloquy, he questions whether ambition is really enough to get him through:

> ...*I have no spur*
> *To prick the sides of my intent, but only*
> *Vaulting ambition, which o'erleaps itself*
> *And falls on th'other.*

The mixed metaphor Macbeth uses imagines his murderous purpose as a horse: he has no motive (spur) other than ambition to carry him on towards this goal, and is worried that this ambition will carry (vault) him too far, as if jumping onto a horse and falling off the other side.

So, like his wife rightly says, ambition is nothing without 'the illness should attend it'. We can all be ambitious, but unless we turn that into action it remains as some vague aspiration. How many people do we know who that applies to? It usually ends up with frustration and bitterness.

Let this be a lesson to you all: be ambitious, but do something about it. Don't just dream. Also, don't murder any kings in the process. Free advice! You're welcome.

TOO MUCH AMBITION CAN BE A DANGEROUS THING

If you were going to sum up the message of the play in eight words, it would be these. All of Shakespeare's tragic plays, like all the plays of the period, have an instructional (pedagogical) function as well as an entertainment function. They all have a moral.

At its most basic, his tragedies all show that too much of one quality ends in tragedy/death. With Hamlet it's overthinking, with Othello it's excessive, possessive love and its accompanying jealousy, and with Romeo it's being too much of a romantic and not enough of a realist.

With Macbeth, the moral is that too much ambition can only ever end badly. This is what drives the couple through the first half of the play, and it's what finally drives Lady Macbeth mad when she loses her husband to the power that consumes him.

In Act 3 Scene 1, Macbeth clearly shows that it isn't enough just to be king - this ambition has only taken him so far:

> *To be thus is nothing, but to be safely thus. (Act 3 Scene 1)*

This is the danger of ambition: you could say it never has an end. We can think we reach our goal only to realise that there are further goals beyond. In itself this isn't a bad thing - it keeps us moving on, keeps us hungry.

But at its most negative it can drive people into more and more negative behaviour. Macbeth is only beginning: by the end he will have the blood of many on his hands as he attempts to hold onto a crown that was never rightly his in the first place.

So, be ambitious, but don't let it rule your life. More free advice!

MASCULINITY AND FEMININITY

So much of Shakespeare's Canon deals with the relationship between men and women. And, what you will see, is that men win. Always. There are no exceptions.

What do you mean, I hear you cry. *Men always win*? Yes, that was life in Shakespeare's day (and right up until about 100 years ago when the Suffragettes started to change things for the better).

Women had severely limited rights, owned nothing, and were the property of their father before being handed to another man through marriage.

That's why even today the marriage ceremony uses language like 'do you take this woman' and why the father of the bride 'gives away' his daughter at the start of the ceremony.

So when I say 'men always win' it's because Shakespeare's plays, through how they present both men and women, reinforced to the society of the time that women were not to get any big ideas or try to be powerful as it will always end up badly for them (or they will end up married - it depends on the play).

It might seem on first glance like a character such as Beatrice in *Much Ado About Nothing* keeps her humour and strong character to the end, but the truth is she gives herself to Benedick and is submissive and much, much quieter at the end (at the start of the play she talks a lot).

So even the strongest women lose something of themselves in the end. This is what I mean by the men always winning.

Don't think of it as bad, or wrong. It's just how it was at the time. It's easy to look through the lens of the 21st Century when we read plays like *Macbeth* and *Much Ado* and get really angry with how women were treated.

I think this is a mistake. Just see it as society working out how best to operate. These things take time, and thankfully we are in a far better position nowadays.

A few examples of what happen to women in Shakespeare's Tragedies:

In *Othello*, Desdemona is accused of having an affair (only she's not, it's just that Othello is a jealous type and his 'friend' Iago convinces him that she's being unfaithful). Othello smothers her with a pillow but even on her death bed she pins the blame on herself and tells everyone she committed suicide just before she dies.

In *Hamlet*, Ophelia is treated terribly by Hamlet, who she loves. She goes mad and drowns herself.

In *Macbeth*, once Lady Macbeth loses her husband to the power that takes him over, she goes mad with guilt and kills herself.

See a pattern, anyone?

So when we analyse masculinity and femininity in the play we need to bear in mind that Shakespeare was a product of the time in history in which he was writing. It doesn't necessarily make him a mysoginist (someone who hates women). It just makes him Elizabethan.

MASCULINITY AND HONOUR

Being a man is all about being honourable, and we see Macbeth move from a position of great honour to even greater dishonour as the play progresses.

There is a lot of talk of honour from the start: in Act 1 Scene 2 Macdonwald is called a 'rebel's whore' for rebelling against the King. Look at the language used here: lack of honour is associated with being a prostitute: not male, but female.

The soldier, when he finishes recounting what happened on the battlefield, is told by King Duncan 'So well thy words become thee as thy wounds; / They smack of honour both.' Both his injuries and his words show the King how honourable this soldier is. To speak the truth and to fight for the King are the ultimate in male honour.

This is why Macbeth is made Thane of Cawdor: he takes this title from Macdonwald and with it the honour attached. His bravery on the battlefield is rewarded by Duncan: his strength in defeating the rebel shows his honour.

However, as the play progresses, this honour is rapidly destroyed through his selfish, power-hungry actions. Being honourable is about showing good character, being trustworthy, a man of your word.

All of these things relate to how to act towards others. As soon as Macbeth murders Duncan any hope of being honourable is destroyed, as he does this for no other reason than his own desire for power and control.

If Duncan had been a terrible tyrant, then it would have been different. After all, Macduff kills King Macbeth at the end of the play, and he and his fellow thanes are made earls for doing so, 'the first that ever Scotland / in such an honour named.' (Act 5, Scene 8).

Honour therefore is linked to motivation (and this is a good lesson for us all). If we act in a way that is for the good of those around us, and do not behave purely out of selfish reasons, then our actions will be honourable. It's the best way to live.

Remember that we are looking at honour linked to masculinity here: it is Lady Macbeth who initially acts in the most dishonourable way, pushing Macbeth to murder the King when he initially has second thoughts. In Act 1 Scene 7, Macbeth says;

> *We will proceed no further in this business:*
> *He hath honoured me of late; and I have bought*
> *Golden opinions from all sorts of people*

Lady Macbeth throws this honour back in his face, saying it is not manly to go back on his word: 'When you durst do it, then you were a man'. As far as Lady Macbeth is concerned, this honour is worthless if he does not use his closeness to the King to get what she believes they both deserve. Honour means nothing unless you have the power and status that go with it.

Remember also it is the female witches who first plant the seed by prophesying his future. Therefore, the key challenges to male honour in the play initially come from the female characters.

MASCULINITY AND AMBITION

We've already looked at ambition in the last section, but I think it's worth examining it in the light of what it shows us about masculinity.

The most ambitious character in the first Act of the play is undoubtedly Lady Macbeth. Why then is she a good example of ambition linking to masculinity?

Because she explicitly denies her female sexuality in order to make room for the male qualities she needs to succeed in their plan. In act 1 Scene 5, Lady Macbeth shows her concern that Macbeth has ambition but not the 'illness should attend it': he has the desire but not the cold-blooded qualities needed in order to succeed.

Her immortal soliloquy, where she asks the spirits to 'unsex me here', shows how she recognises that any female qualities will only stand in her way. She does not want any 'compunctious visitings of nature' to block her: her human nature as a woman needs to be denied access.

The brutal images of her inviting evil spirits to take her 'milk for gall' shows just how much she wants to remove anything kind or nurturing from her body. Breast milk, the giver of life, must turn into something bitter in order for her to achieve her goals.

THE ROLE OF WOMEN IN THE PLAY

I've already mentioned how women in Shakespeare generally get a rough deal (in my opinion Lady Macbeth gets off lightly: in *Titus Andronicus*, Lavinia is raped and has her tongue cut out and hands chopped off so she cannot name her rapists. Yes, that was written in the 16th Century!).

However, and as I have said before, it is worth thinking about the function/purpose of the women in the play as it is a very masculine play - probably Shakespeare's most masculine.

There are only five women: Lady Macbeth, Lady Macduff, and the three witches. All are very different representations of femininity. There is no Mrs Duncan, or Mrs Banquo, and no reference to the mothers of Macbeth or Lady Macbeth. As I've mentioned, it is a very male play.

What is most apparent throughout this play (as in all others) is that women who transgress/step outside of what society expects of them are, quite frankly, doomed.

Whilst plays like Macbeth are primarily created to entertain, they also serve a moral/educational purpose: I mentioned this in the introduction when I talked about the Gunpowder Plot. The audience, continually seeing 'unruly' women being punished, will understand that society expects women to act in a certain way.

Lady Macbeth

Lady Macbeth is generally not a 'doer' in the play: the only thing she does is take the daggers back to Duncan's bedchamber and smear the grooms with his blood. Other than that, it is all Macbeth. All she has is her influence over her husband: it is through him that she can become great. Her words are her biggest weapons.

And it is because she loses her influence that she loses her mind. The tipping point is in Act 3 Scene 2, Lady Macbeth asks what has happened to Banquo. Macbeth's response - 'be innocent of the knowledge, dearest chuck' could almost be seen as patronising: he no longer wants her to have an active part to play in his pursuit of absolute power.

Without a voice, without a role to play, there is no longer a purpose for Lady Macbeth. This is important: *women cannot be defined in any way other than in relationship to the men in their lives.* (I thought it worth putting into italics.)

Lady Macbeth has a purpose when she is working alongside her husband. When he no longer needs her, she loses her reason to live. She is, after all, Lady Macbeth. She does not have her own name.

It's the same with Ophelia in Hamlet - he rejects her totally and she goes mad. She cannot live if she is not defined in relation to Hamlet. She may have her own name but she has no individual identity.

Lady Macduff

Lady Macduff is a totally different representation of femininity. She is far more stereotypical: in Act 4 Scene 2 she shows her fear at being left alone in the castle. She refers to herself and her son as 'the most diminutive of birds': weak and helpless.

The bird metaphor runs through this scene - when the messenger tells her to leave the castle as she is danger, she says 'whither should I fly?' She has no defence against the approaching murderers.

We don't see her death: she is murdered 'off scene' as most characters are in Shakespeare. This is where we get the word 'obscene' - something too grotesque or unpleasant to look at.

What is her role? That's simple: to spur Macduff on to get back to Scotland and revenge the death of his family. When he hears of their murder he cannot believe it: 'What, all my pretty chickens and their dam / At one fell swoop?' (Act 4 Scene 3).

The bird metaphor seeks to continually remind us that these were innocent, weak victims - the worst and most dishonourable thing for Macbeth to do was to murder a wife and her children.

So, as well as providing Macduff with the motivation to kill Macbeth, it also reminds us of how far Macbeth has fallen.

The Witches

The Witches are a good example of what happens to women when they remain totally outside the world that men define for them.

They are bearded, ugly, and sinister. They live on the 'blasted heath', on the outskirts of society. They are unwelcome and untrusted. A reminder to women watching the play that not being part of the world of men can lead to being banished to the edge of society.

So, as well as their narrative function in the play, they serve as a warning. If you don't conform to what men expect of you, and seek power in your own terms, you will be cast out and branded a witch.

FORM AND STRUCTURE

THE DRAMATIC FORM

When you read a play like *Macbeth*, it's important to pay close attention to how the words are set out on the page. In this way, reading a play is a little like reading a poem.

Generally, Shakespeare has his characters speaking in blank verse in *Macbeth*. Each line has ten syllables, uses iambic pentameter (ten syllables, one unstressed syllable followed by a stressed syllable), but does not rhyme. My personal favourite comes at the end of the play, when Macbeth is debating the futility of life:

> *Tomorrow, and tomorrow, and tomorrow,*
> *Creeps in this petty pace from day to day,*
> *To the last syllable of recorded time;*
> *And all our yesterdays have lighted fools*
> *The way to dusty death. Out, out, brief candle!*
> *Life's but a walking shadow, a poor player,*
> *That struts and frets his hour upon the stage,*
> *And then is heard no more. It is a tale*
> *Told by an idiot, full of sound and fury,*
> *Signifying nothing. (Act 5, Scene 5)*

Why does he use this technique? It is generally to make the characters seem important, of high status and intelligence. Speaking in blank verse gives the language authority and weight. You can't really speak trivially when you are using blank verse.

The exceptions to the use of blank verse are the prose used in the Porter's scene (as we have seen before), and when Macbeth speaks to the murderers. It is as if Macbeth doesn't want to waste such poetic language on low status characters.

Why is it useful to know this? Because if you're able to point to specific language techniques Shakespeare uses to emphasise certain elements of the text and suggest the status of certain characters, you're on your way to the top grades as not many students do this.

HOW DO YOU DO IT?

Here's an example of how you might refer to a technique such as iambic pentameter when analysing the soliloquy above:

> The opening lines of Macbeth's soliloquy point to his growing disillusionment with life. The repetition of 'tomorrow' is emphasised through the use of iambic pentameter: the slow, alternating beat of each word slowing the reading down and making the words themselves sound laborious. This is further emphasised in the second line: the emphasis on 'in…pet…pace…day…day' making Macbeth sound exhausted as he speaks.

Try to throw in the occasional reference to language techniques and you can't go far wrong. Just make sure you *always* say what effect they have - don't only refer to blank verse - say why it's used.

THE FIVE ACT STRUCTURE

A quick one on structure…

Shakespeare's Tragedies typically follow *Freytag's Pyramid of Dramatic Structure*. It consists of five parts:

1. **Exposition**: this introduces important elements into the play and can give clues as to what is to follow. In *Macbeth*, the opening scenes introduce us to the Macbeths, prophecy the future without saying how it will be realised, and begin to flesh out the Macbeths' plans.
2. **Rising action**. At the beginning of this section (or at the end of the Exposition), an inciting incident kicks off the drama proper. In this case it is the murder of Duncan. This sets in process a chain of events that rise in drama (hence the title) and lead towards the climax. In *Macbeth*, the murder is followed by a series of increasingly awful actions, leading to the final scene in Macbeth's castle.
3. **Climax**. This is sometimes called the 'dramatic centre'. This is the turning point in the play that changes the protagonist's fate and is the result of the events that occurred through the rising action. What we notice is that

the protagonist, the closer he gets to the climax, the less control he has over events. In the case of *Macbeth*, the climax is the escape of Fleance. As it has been prophesied that Banquo's son will become King, his escape begins a downward spiral for Macbeth, who becomes increasingly paranoid as he loses control. We know that at this point he is doomed.

4. **Falling action**. From the climax it's downhill all the way for Macbeth. Malcolm and Macduff draw closer to the castle and Macbeth prepares to fight. Shakespeare sets up the falling action beautifully: Malcolm had to escape to England on his father's death so had to return to take his rightful place as king once he assembled an army. Macduff had to avenge his wife. Fleance's escape was needed to give Macbeth a reason for his increasing paranoia.

5. **Catastrophe/Tragic End**: like *Romeo and Juliet*, *Macbeth* has a double tragedy at the end: the death of both Macbeths. One dies by their own hand, the other by the hand of the avenger. Malcolm is crowned King and a new order is established.

You may be asking why it's important to know this. Like knowing a little about why Shakespeare uses blank verse, if you're able to refer to the different structural elements of the play when analysing, you'll pick up extra marks.

So, rather than saying 'At the start of the play, we see…' say 'At the play's exposition, we see….'

It's not hard to do, but examiners love it! Most are frustrated playwrights/novelists/poets and self-confessed language geeks so the more technical stuff you can add in, the better.

TACKLING THE EXAM

ASSESSMENT OBJECTIVES AND MARK SCHEME

As you'll have seen in my other books (and if you haven't then do check them out), I like to show you how to tackle some typical exam questions.

It's vital to have a good working knowledge of the play, to know who said what and when, but unless you can craft a clear, logical answer you'll have the examiner scratching their head trying to work out how to award you marks.

For, as I have said so many times before (and never get bored of saying it), writing exam answers is a game. If you know the rules up front you've a good chance of getting excellent marks. If you think you can wing it on the day, chances are you'll fall flat on your face. Or other part of your anatomy.

The AQA GCSE question on Macbeth will give you a passage from the play and pose you a question. We'll look at some examples in the next section.

A WORD ON THE DREADED AOS...

I know how you probably feel whenever anyone mentions Assessment Objectives. You probably feel a little cold inside or sick in your mouth. Or maybe you just glaze over a bit. Whatever your reaction, it's worth spending a few moments looking at them as they can help. Honestly they can.

No, really. Trust me.

Here are the AOs for the Macbeth question:

AO1: Read, understand and respond to texts. You should be able to:

- maintain a critical style and develop an informed personal response
- use textual references, including quotations, to support and illustrate interpretations.

AO2: Analyse the language, form and structure used by a writer to create meanings and effects, using relevant subject terminology where appropriate.

AO3: Show understanding of the relationships between texts and the contexts in which they were written.

AO4: Use a range of vocabulary and sentence structures, for clarity, purpose and effect, with accurate spelling and punctuation.

Let's change them into human speak:

AO1: Write intelligent, detailed things about the play, bringing in your own ideas and using quotations.

AO2: Make sure you write about the play as a play - talk about blank verse, iambic pentameter, rising action etc.

AO3: Have something to say about the historical period Shakespeare was writing in and how it impacted on his writing of the play.

No one writes in a vacuum (or any other household appliance for that matter).

AO4: Watch your spelling, use paragraphs etc.

Hold those four objectives in your head when you write and you can't go far wrong. Just think of them as the ingredients for excellent essay writing.

I'll refer to the AOs throughout this Chapter.

THE MARK SCHEME

Marks are broken down like this:

- AO1: 12 marks
- AO2: 12 marks
- AO3: 6 marks
- AO4: 4 marks

30 marks in total with an additional 4 bonus marks for spelling, punctuation, grammar, layout etc.

So, analysing and writing about structure is twice as important as the historical context bit. You should therefore aim to write twice as much about the first two AOs.

AO4 should just happen if you plan well and don't rush and make silly mistakes.

GRADE BOUNDARIES

The exam board give examiners a guide for what to look for when they're marking against the AOs. It's helpful before we look at sample questions and answers to see what these are.

A LOW GRADE (3-4)

Students who get around a Grade 4 will write **a few generally relevant comments** on the text but will tend to lapse in retelling the story (AO1).

They will **identify some of the methods** the writer uses but are unlikely to say much about the effect they have (AO2).

They have **some awareness of context** but find it hard to link this to the text (AO3).

They are **inconsistent with their spelling etc** and write with simple sentences without much variety (AO4).

A MID GRADE (5-6)

Students who get around a Grade 5-6 will write a **clear response with suitable references** (AO1).

They will make **clear references to the writer's methods** to support their points (AO2).

Clear links will made with some aspects of historical context (AO3).

Spelling and punctuation is **generally pretty good** and there's a **wider range** of sentences and vocabulary (AO4).

A GOOD GRADE (7-8)

This will show **very effective understanding** and careful use of references and quotes (AO1).

It will **analyse carefully and comment consistently well, interpreting** ideas (AO2).

Very effective links will be made between context and text (AO3).

Spelling etc. will be **generally excellent** (AO4).

AN EXCELLENT GRADE (8-9)

This will show a **broad, conceptualised idea** of the text, backed up by **well-judged and wide-ranging references and quotations** (AO1).

It will **analyse and explore** texts precisely and convincingly. There will be **finely tuned comment** on language, form and structure (AO2).

A **wide range of contextual factors** will be convincingly and relevantly written about (AO3).

Spelling etc will be **very accurate** and meaning will be **clearly controlled** (AO4).

KEY WORDS TO FOCUS ON

As you can see, there are certain key words that stand out depending on the level you're writing at:

- **Low** answers will be basic, making some relevant responses and referring to some writing features. However, these answers tend towards retelling chunks of the text rather than analysing. (If you're not sure what I mean by analysing don't worry: I'll come on to that.)
- **Mid** answers will be clearer in both their response and reference to methods, and will generally be well written.
- **Good** answers will show analysis - understanding themes and ideas exploring the effect of writer's methods.
- **Excellent** answers will be controlled, detailed, intelligent, insightful and very well written. They will go deeply into the text and show originality and flair.

Of course you want to be writing excellent answers! Let's see if I can show you how to do that in the next section.

HOW TO APPROACH AN EXAM PAPER

Here's a sample question for us to get our teeth stuck into. It's taken from the specimen paper you can find on the AQA website

Section A: Shakespeare

Answer **one** question from this section on your chosen text.

Read the following extract from Act 1 Scene 5 of *Macbeth* and then answer the question that follows.

At this point in the play Lady Macbeth is speaking. She has just received the news that King Duncan will be spending the night at her castle.

> *The raven himself is hoarse*
> *That croaks the fatal entrance of Duncan*
> *Under my battlements. Come, you spirits*
> *That tend on mortal thoughts, unsex me here,*
> *And fill me from the crown to the toe topfull*
> *Of direst cruelty; make thick my blood,*
> *Stop up th'access and passage to remorse*
> *That no compunctious visitings of nature*
> *Shake my fell purpose nor keep peace between*

> *Th'effect and it. Come to my woman's breasts,*
> *And take my milk for gall, you murd'ring ministers,*
> *Wherever in your sightless substances*
> *You wait on nature's mischief. Come, thick night,*
> *And pall thee in the dunnest smoke of hell,*
> *That my keen knife see not the wound it makes*
> *Nor heaven peep through the blanket of the dark,*
> *To cry 'Hold, hold!'*

Starting with this speech, explain how far you think Shakespeare presents Lady Macbeth as a powerful woman.

Write about:

how Shakespeare presents Lady Macbeth in this speech

how Shakespeare presents Lady Macbeth in the play as a whole.

[30 marks]

AO4 [4 marks]

MARK SCHEME IN MORE DETAIL

The mark scheme gives you additional information: it's quite useful so do check it out as it can show you what the examiner will be looking for.

AO1

- Power in terms of status
- Lady Macbeth's power in terms of her relationship
- Lady Macbeth as a powerful/effective character in the play
- How Lady Macbeth changes as the play develops
- Contrast between Act 1 and Act 3 and/or Act 5

AO2

- How Shakespeare uses Lady Macbeth to influence the plot development

- The use of language to suggest Lady Macbeth's desperation for power
- The use and effect of imagery of the supernatural
- The use and effect of pronouns to suggest power and control

AO3

- Ideas about power and how it is achieved/perceived
- Ideas about the role of women
- Attitudes towards the supernatural
- Ideas about the soul/heaven and hell
- Ideas about equality/status
- Contemporary reception towards Lady Macbeth's behaviour in this speech and
- actions elsewhere in the play

HOW TO TACKLE THIS QUESTION

Here's a foolproof way of tackling this in the exam. You can use this approach for any character-based question.

- First of all, make sure you understand exactly what the question is asking of you. I'd always suggest **underlining the key words**, and making sure that every single thing you write in response refers in some way to those words. In this case it is about how far you think Lady Macbeth is presented as a powerful woman. Not just that she is presented as a powerful woman, but *how far*. So you can say how she may not be so powerful, which makes sense as the play progresses. These small details are important!
- Make sure you know how long you have to answer this question so you don't overrun and not leave yourself enough time for the other questions on the paper. You have 1 hour 45 minutes to answer two questions. I would suggest you aim for 45 minutes per question with the other 15 minutes broken down into:

- 5 minutes reading the paper carefully at the beginning (and doing some breathing)
- 10 minutes checking over your answers at the end so you don't make any crazy mistakes.
- Now, you'll focus in on the exam paper passage. Underline anything which refers to Lady Macbeth being powerful. Nothing else: just any words and phrases which suggest power to us.
- Next, you'll go through the play and find other examples which show her being powerful. Underline them and make a note of the page reference *on your answer paper*. Don't worry too much at this point about Act, Scene and Line numbers - just jot down the page reference and a brief note as to how it answers the question. The reason you want to put all your planning on your answer paper is that if you run out of time the examiner may still give you marks if you make relevant notes. Remember to look at the formal elements as well - if it's written in blank verse, particular uses of punctuation maybe or line breaks. Anything which adds to your understanding of how Lady Macbeth seems powerful.
- I'd then suggest you jot down a **quick paragraph plan** so you know the order in which you'll write. Chronologically (order of zvents) is perfectly fine with character studies - in fact I'd usually suggest this as it makes it easier to show how a character might change (which is very much the case with Lady Macbeth as she loses power as the play progresses). It might look something like this:

- *First impressions - first things she says, how she appears to Macbeth*
- *How she convinces Macbeth to do the deed. Her reaction to Macbeth when he murders the king*
- *Macbeth's response to her when she asks him about Banquo*
- *How she acts during the banqueting scene and how this shows her losing power*
- *How she ends the play and why (loss of power, madness)*

- 4-5 paragraphs is enough for an exam essay like this. Writing this short plan will help keep you focused, as everything you write in that paragraph will link to the subject of the paragraph and the key words in the question. Notice I don't include an introduction or conclusion? In an exam, with a limited amount of time, I would always suggest getting straight into the analysis. Introductions can often look like the candidate is writing their way into the exam. But because you've done a paragraph plan there'll be no chance of that happening with you, will there.
- Begin every paragraph with a **short, punchy sentence** which shows the examiner exactly what you're going to be writing about in that paragraph and helps keep you on track:
- *'In the passage, Lady Macbeth is presented as a woman with immense power.'*
- *'When we are first introduced to Lady Macbeth we are presented with a woman concerned that her husband won't have the strength to become king.'*
- *'Lady Macbeth shows her strength and power both before and after Duncan's murder.'*
- For those of you who've read my English Language book (do give it a go - I think it's quite useful), you'll know I have a certain way of structuring analysis. You'll probably have heard of PEE - Point, Evidence, Explanation - and that's ok. However, I prefer **PEAL - Point, Evidence, Analysis, Link**. Why? Because it's important that you show how your ideas develop throughout the paragraph. An examiner will be looking at this carefully. If you offer one quote and say one thing about it, you're looking at a 4 or 5. If you say 2-3 things, adding detail and **making links between quotes**, you'll be moving up to the 6,7 or more.
- Remember that you are writing a literature essay, not a language essay. And as such you have to make sure you include something on **context**. In this case you'd be referring to the typical role and representation of women

and how Lady Macbeth goes against this (and what happens to her as a result). Don't forget that AO3 context is worth 6 marks.
- The other key thing to make sure you do is write about the techniques Shakespeare uses. You need to make sure you use the right terminology: metaphor/figurative language, simile and so on. This is part of AO2 and is worth 12 marks.

Ok, let's see this in action…

SAMPLE ESSAY PARAGRAPHS

It's time to look at a few examples. I won't write entire essays below, but rather share with you a few paragraphs and ask you to suggest what sort of grade they might get. You can refer back to the last section and imagine you are the examiner. What evidence do you see that would get the student a particular grade?

Remember - these aren't whole essays - just sample paragraphs.

Example 1

Lady Macbeth is a powerful woman in the play. In this section she is talking about not wanting to be a woman anymore and being filled with crulety. When she says 'come you spirits' she means that she wants evil spirits to come to her. This is because she needs some help from them. This is before they murder Duncan.

After this she talks about her woman's breasts and mudering ministers. She ends the speech by wanting night to come so no one can see what they do. She wants to be unsexed because at the time women had no rights so she doesn't think being a woman will allow her to kill the king.

Example 2

In this passage from the play, Lady Macbeth is summoning evil spirits to give her power. She begins by saying 'come you spirits', as if she is casting a spell to call them to her. She wants them to remove her femininity - she says 'unsex me here' which means she wants them to stop her from feeling anything so she and

Macbeth can murder the king. This is because she thinks that being a woman will make her weaker. This was a common way of thinking at the time the play was written as people didn't see women as being powerful.

The phrase 'make thick my blood' is an interesting one as it suggests her blood needs to be made thicker in order to gain more power to commit the murder. The sounds of the words also add to that feeling as the words themselves sound thick. When she says 'stop up the access and passage to remorse' she wants the spirits to make sure she no longer feels any guilt for killing Duncan.

Example 3

Whilst the play is set in the 11th Century, Lady Macbeth is very much a product of the era in which Shakespeare was writing. She knows that, if she wishes to have the power to go through with the 'deed' she will need to have her femininity removed. This soliloquy, which comes just before the arrival of Macbeth back to the castle, is a potent reminder of how weak women were seen in general, and therefore how much they relied on the supernatural in order to gain the power they did not inherently possess.

She begins by summoning up the 'spirits who tend on mortal thoughts' and demands 'unsex me here': in order to summon up this power she needs to have her femininity removed. It is not a request, it is a demand: she is not acting in any way as one would expect a woman of the time to act.

Language like 'direst cruelty' and 'make thick my blood' are deeply sinister, the sounds of the words themselves adding to this effect: the consonance of 'make thick' is particularly effective. She equates 'remorse' with being female: she wants this to be stopped up as she sees this as a part of female 'nature' that she has to have removed. It is only in this way that she will gain the power she so desperately craves.

Three responses, three very different grades. Have you worked them out?

If I was an examiner, I would give the first around a Grade 4, the second around a Grade 6, and if Student 3 carried on like that they'd be on their way to a Grade 8 or 9 no question.

Let's dig into them in a bit more detail and see where marks were picked up, and indeed dropped…

EXAMPLE 1

...is clearly written, doesn't use any complex language, and does show some understanding: the second sentence shows that. There is evidence of using quotations and a basic understanding of what the quotation means. However, the second half of the paragraph lapses into retelling the plot, with no explanation. There is a little evidence of context but it feels like the candidate has stuck this at the end because they remembered they had to. It is also not very well linked back into the play: women's rights and killing kings don't necessarily go together. There are a couple of spelling mistakes in there as well.

EXAMPLE 2

...is a little better: it shows a more detailed understanding of the play, uses quotes more effectively, and begins to analyse: phrases such as 'as if' and 'this is because' are examples of what I call 'analytical signposts' - indicators to the examiner that you are about to explain the quote in some depth (more on that below). The candidate mentions some language techniques but there is no technical language used. There is some relevant contextual detail but it's a little superficial ('a common way of thinking at the time': Which time? What way of thinking?)

EXAMPLE 3

...is as good as you'd get at GCSE - in fact if I read this I'd think this person was ready for A-Level. I don't say this to put you off, but rather to give you the ingredients so you can give the top grade your best shot. I like the way the paragraph begins with context that frames everything that follows. It is specific - the candidate places the representation of women both within the historical period of the play but also the time in which it was written. There is technical language in there (soliloquy, consonance), and the analysis is excellent - every time the candidate says one thing, they say something more - the reference to the demand, specific detail about language techniques. They show real control of how to use quotation, taking individual words and weaving them into their sentences. The paragraph ends with a simple yet insightful closing comment. Language is sophisticated throughout: inherently, summoning, craves.

Why don't we now look at how to craft the Grade 8-9 paragraph in even more depth? I thought that would make you happy.

WRITING KILLER PARAGRAPHS: 5 TIPS

Drum roll: the moment you've been waiting for. Below I give you a few tips for how to write killer paragraphs. I refer to this in a previous section but it's worth really picking out the most useful ingredients of top essays.

If you use these tips, do lots of practice essays, and make sure you know the play text back to front (which if you have read my guide and made notes in your play you will have done), I can pretty well guarantee you an improved grade.

What I can't (sadly) do is guarantee you a Grade 9: it is safe to say that some candidates just have more natural ability and are able to say more original things than others.

However, if you follow these ingredients you will have a far firmer foundation on which to excel, and are therefore more likely to achieve these top grades. So, give yourself every chance and follow these steps.

Here are the top 5 things to remember!

1. SAY A LOT ABOUT A LITTLE, RATHER THAN A LITTLE ABOUT A LOT.

I wasn't taught this until I reached university but wish someone had told me sooner! It is far better to take a few small details and say as much as you can about them, rather than try to write about an entire passage or quote a long piece of text.

In fact, I would go as far as to say that Grade 9 essays tend to quote no more than 4-5 words at any one time, as this forces you to go deep.

As an example, take the final section of the passage:

> *Come, thick night,*
> *And pall thee in the dunnest smoke of hell,*
> *That my keen knife see not the wound it makes*
> *Nor heaven peep through the blanket of the dark,*
> *To cry 'Hold, hold!'*

Now, a Grade 5 or 6 candidate might quote the whole thing, which is rather a waste of time as the examiner also has the passage in front of them (bet you didn't know that... oh, you did). It's much better to pick out key words and feed them into your analysis, and say as much as you possibly can about them. Think about all three AOs when you're writing as if you can say three things about a short quote you're on a winner!

You obviously won't do this for every single quote, but it's worth seeing if you can extend your ideas just that bit further each time:

Lady Macbeth ends her soliloquy by asking the 'thick night' to cover her so that her 'keen knife see not the wound it makes'. 'Thick' in this context refers to the night being unfeeling: by personifying night she seems to suggest that the night becomes an accomplice in her crime, hiding her from being discovered. She additionally personifies the knife, again suggesting that it will not be her who does the killing, that the knife itself will be the guilty one. The reference to 'heaven peeping' insinuates that heaven is somehow weak: there is no strength in peeping - it is the sort of thing nervous people do. This binary between heaven and hell, with hell clearly winning on this occasion, is one that dominated the historical period, so the audience would fully understand what Lady Macbeth was alluding to.

I would hope by now you could see all the good stuff going on here. The candidate takes their analysis as far as they can, building one sentence on another.

2. USE PUNCTUATION CLEVERLY TO INDICATE YOU ARE ABOUT TO ANALYSE

This one is super easy to do but very effective. Use a colon (:) or dash (-) to show that you are about to analyse. You can see both of these in the passage above - check them out. You begin by placing the quote in context, then explore your ideas after the mark of punctuation:

'Thick' in this context refers to the night being unfeeling: by personifying night she seems to suggest that the night becomes an accomplice in her crime, hiding her from being discovered.

The reference to 'heaven peeping' insinuates that heaven is somehow weak: there is no strength in peeping - it is the sort of thing nervous people do.

3. USE SPECIFIC LANGUAGE TO SHOW YOU ARE ANALYSING

As I mentioned in an earlier section, I refer to these as analytical signposts. They are an easy way to say to the examiner 'hey, look what I'm doing, I'm analysing, please give me a higher grade'.

These are some good phrases to use:

This suggests...

This shows us...

This refers to...

The writer seems to suggest...

This insinuates...

You can see a number of these in the answer above.

4. USE AS BROAD A VOCABULARY AS POSSIBLE BUT KEEP IT CLEAR: DON'T DISAPPEAR UP YOUR OWN BACKSIDE

Sounds painful? Imagine an examiner having to read countless essays that are trying to sound clever but end up making no sense. Keep your writing clear and precise, but don't be afraid to use as broad a vocabulary as possible: examples above include 'accomplice', 'alluding' and 'binary'.

5. USE PHRASES TO SHOW POTENTIALLY DIFFERENT READINGS OF THE SAME QUOTE

This will take you into the 8s and 9s. Don't just settle for one analysis, think about how quotes can be read in different ways. You can use these phrases to signpost that you are examining alternative points of view:

One the other hand,

Conversely,

However,

One reading could be…. but another suggests….

Remember that different people can read texts in different ways: how we read Macbeth would differ hugely from how someone in the early 17th Century would have read it. If you're exploring things like the difference between male and female you could certainly refer to a modern reading in opposition to how someone in the 17th Century would have interpreted it.

PRACTICE PAPERS

YOUR TURN - TIME TO PRACTISE

So that you can have a go at practicing everything I've taught you (I know there's a lot to take in but don't worry, just take one Act at a time), here are some questions I made up or that are cribbed from various sources online.

QUESTION 1

Read the following extract from Act I Scene 7 of *Macbeth* and then answer the question that follows.

At this point in the play, Macbeth is speaking. He is in inner turmoil over the decision to kill King Duncan:

> *He's here in double trust:*
> *First, as I am his kinsman and his subject,*
> *Strong both against the deed; then, as his host,*
> *Who should against his murderer shut the door,*
> *Not bear the knife myself. Besides, this Duncan*

> *Hath borne his faculties so meek, hath been*
> *So clear in his great office, that his virtues*
> *Will plead like angels, trumpet-tongued, against*
> *The deep damnation of his taking-off;*
> *And Pity, like a naked new-born babe*
> *Striding the blast, or heaven's cherubim, horsed*
> *Upon the sightless curriers of the air,*
> *Shall blow the horrid deed in every eye,*
> *That tears shall drown the wind. I have no spur*
> *To prick the sides of my intent*
> *but only Vaulting ambition, which o'erleaps itself*
> *And falls on the other.*

Starting with this speech, explore how Shakespeare presents the theme of inner conflict. Write about:

- how Shakespeare presents the theme of inner conflict in this speech
- how Shakespeare presents the theme of inner conflict in the play as a whole.

QUESTION 2

Read the following extract from Act 5 Scene 5 of *Macbeth* and then answer the question that follows.

At this point in the play, Macbeth is speaking. He has just discovered that Lady Macbeth has killed herself and is questioning life itself:

> *To-morrow, and to-morrow, and to-morrow,*
> *Creeps in this petty pace from day to day*
> *To the last syllable of recorded time,*
> *And all our yesterdays have lighted fools*
> *The way to dusty death. Out, out, brief candle!*
> *Life's but a walking shadow, a poor player*
> *That struts and frets his hour upon the stage*

> *And then is heard no more: it is a tale*
> *Told by an idiot, full of sound and fury,*
> *Signifying nothing.*

Starting with this speech, explore how Shakespeare presents the theme of death. Write about:

- how Shakespeare presents the theme of death in this speech
- how Shakespeare presents the theme of death in the play as a whole.

QUESTION 3

Read the following extract from Act 1 Scene 7 of *Macbeth* and then answer the question that follows.

At this point in the play, Macbeth has told Lady Macbeth that they will no longer go through with the murder of King Duncan:

> *What beast was't, then,*
> *That made you break this enterprise to me?*
> *When you durst do it, then you were a man;*
> *And, to be more than what you were, you would*
> *Be so much more the man. Nor time nor place*
> *Did then adhere, and yet you would make both:*
> *They have made themselves, and that their fitness now*
> *Does unmake you. I have given suck, and know*
> *How tender 'tis to love the babe that milks me:*
> *I would, while it was smiling in my face,*
> *Have pluck'd my nipple from his boneless gums,*
> *And dash'd the brains out, had I so sworn as you*
> *Have done to this.*

Starting with this speech, explore how Shakespeare presents the theme of masculinity and femininity. Write about:

- how Shakespeare presents the theme of masculinity and femininity in this speech
- how Shakespeare presents the theme of masculinity and femininity in the play as a whole.

HOW TO CREATE USEFUL REVISION MATERIALS

Well done! You've got to the end of the play, made lots of notes, annotated your play text, practised some questions, and are now ready to revise.

But wait: how do you do revise efficiently? There's a useful technique I'd like to share with you which I hope will help. Follow this plan to maximise your time.

1. REMIND YOURSELF OF THE ASSESSMENT OBJECTIVES AND MARK SCHEME

First of all, take the time to remind yourself of what you'll be examined on. Go back through the section on AOs from earlier in this book and list the key words. It might look something like this:

- AO1 - close reading of the play, small details, analysis, quotes
- AO2 - Language used, layout, fact it's a play so you need to write about it as a play with performers etc.
- AO3 - Social historical context - say something about the time it was written and how this informs characters and action

- AO4 - Make sure answer is clearly laid out and focus on spelling and keeping handwriting legible.

Now, as you compile your notes, you can keep these in mind. The more you remember them the more likely you are to make sure everything you revise for falls into one of these buckets.

Look again at the sorts of things you'll be marked on with specific questions. For example, if we look back at the question on Lady Macbeth, we can see the areas the examiner wants to focus on:

•AO1

- Power in terms of **status**
- Lady Macbeth's power in terms of her **relationship**
- Lady Macbeth as a **powerful/effective character** in the play
- How Lady Macbeth **changes** as the play develops
- **Contrast** between Act 1 and Act 3 and/or Act 5

AO2

- How Shakespeare uses Lady Macbeth to **influence the plot development**
- The use of **language** to suggest Lady Macbeth's desperation for power
- The use and effect of **imagery** of the supernatural
- The use and effect of **pronouns** to suggest power and control

AO3

- Ideas about **power** and how it is achieved/perceived
- Ideas about the **role of women**
- Attitudes towards the **supernatural**
- Ideas about the **soul/heaven and hell**
- Ideas about **equality/status**

- **Contemporary reception** towards Lady Macbeth's behaviour in this speech and
- actions elsewhere in the play

It will be the same for each character and each exam question.

For the **character-based question**, **AO1** is about what characters say and do, how others react to them, and how characters progress through the play. **AO2** is about how the character is presented - the language used, stage directions etc. **AO3** is about how the writer explores ideas about the world through their writing.

For the **theme based question** it's quite similar:

- **AO1** will want you to explore how the characters respond to the themes of the play. It will ask you to show how characters' actions and reactions illustrate the themes and what this says about them.
- **AO2** asks you to think about how characters are used as dramatic devices to explore the theme being examined (remember back to the opening of the chapter on characters). How their characters are presented, how their actions and reactions explore the theme, and how their emotions illustrate it. You should also remember here that you're writing about a play: so refer to stage directions etc. Not just what they say but also the directions the writer gives the actors.
- **AO3** is all about how the writer treats the theme, and what their wider comments are on it. What are they trying to show about the theme through their writing? Are there any characters that could be seen as metaphors (symbols) of the theme?

The reason this is helpful to do before you start is that you can now structure your revision notes around these headings, so that when you write them up neatly and clearly you know which bucket they fall into. It's honestly a bit of a tick list but don't see that as limiting - it's actually quite liberating to work within a framework.

2. GRAB SOME A4 PRINTER PAPER AND COLOURED PENS

- Next up you're going to grab a decent amount of printer paper (steal some from a parent's home office is my advice - just make sure you don't take it all they might need to print out a report later on). Or if you prefer, use loose leaf lined A4 paper. I prefer the freedom of not having lines but that's just me!
- Take a piece, put the name of a character in bold at the top. Now, go back through your notes and as you do, pick out the **key words and phrases** that you've made a note of that describe the character.
- So, for Macbeth it might be *powerful, envious, physical, warlike, primal, paranoid*
- Now, for each of those words you're going to find some **quotes**. Use each character word as a heading, and list quotes underneath. List each quote in one colour.
- Then, in another colour, write a **short analysis** of what this quote tells you about this aspect of the character's personality.
- Try to keep your analysis short and to the point - you're not writing an essay here, just enough to remind you **how the quote adds detail to the character trait**.
- Now, in another colour, make any notes on what this quote is telling about **social and historical context**. You may also wish to underline the most important words so they really burn into your memory.
- This will form the bulk of your revision work on character. There are only so many character traits that you can pick out, and only so many quotes, so this won't take forever, providing you took the time to go through the play carefully making notes as you did.
- And if you've not done that yet, make sure you do that first. There can be no substitute for close and careful reading of the text.

Why colours? You don't have to, of course, but what you'll find is that, by using the same colours for quotes, analysis and context, you'll train your brain to always ensure you have all three colours as you compile your notes, and even when you're in the exam you'll be reminded of those colours and will ensure you cover all the AOs.

3. NOW, MOVE ON TO THEME

You're going to do the same thing now for the main themes of the play. Put one theme at the top of a new sheet of paper, find your quotes, write a short sentence about them, then add something about context. See character and theme revision as being the same when it comes to formatting your notes.

SHOULD I USE FLASH CARDS?

Flash/revision cards are really popular and can be helpful. The only problem I have with them is that they're quite small, and you can't fit much onto them. However, there are A5 versions which I think are more useful, and if you have small, neat handwriting then they might be a good bet.

However, I think A4 paper is as good as anything as you can hole punch the sheets once you've written them up and put them into a folder which will keep everything neat.

I guess it's up to you which method you prefer!

A FEW FINAL WORDS

INTERPRETATIONS OF THE PLAY

I think it's very important to watch the play. If you can't see a live version, check out the many versions of the play that have been filmed. Here are my personal favourites:

- Roman Polanski's 1971 version starring Jon Finch as Macbeth remains my favourite. It's quite mad, which is just how it should be.
- Michael Bogdanov's 1998 version starring Jon Pertwee is set in more modern times but is pretty authentic to the text.
- Justin Kurtzel's 2015 version starring Michael Fassbender is my favourite recent version. Fassbender is excellent in the role.
- There is one free version on Youtube: The Ian McKellen version from 1979. It's a bit dated but still pretty good. If you put Macbeth into Youtube it's the first result.
- For a short version of the play, check out the Animated Tales version on Youtube.

You can find clips on Youtube or buy/rent the whole movie through most streaming services. I would recommend watching more than one version, as referring to the play in performance is helpful as it helps tick AO2 boxes.

THANKS FOR READING!

I hope this guide has been helpful to you. I hope it's felt like I've been sitting alongside you gently suggesting you might consider making the occasional note in your play text. If you haven't, I suggest you go back through this guide and do so. It will help.

If it's been helpful, please do leave me a review on Amazon. It would be much appreciated.

And do also check out my GCSE English Language revision guide, where I take you step by step through the AQA 9-1 Paper. I've also produced a guide for An Inspector Calls which you may also find useful (if you're doing that play, but buy it anyway just because!)

Best of luck when you enter that murky old world of the examiner's head! Don't be scared. They're human too.

Printed in Great Britain
by Amazon